THAI

THAI

hamlyn

First published in the U.K. in 1998
by Hamlyn an imprint of Octopus Publishing Group Ltd.
Michelin House, 81 Fulham Road, London SW3 6RB

This U.S. edition copyright © 1999 Octopus Publishing Group Ltd.

Reprinted 2003

Printed in China

ISBN 0 600 59872 1

NOTES

Eggs should be medium to large unless otherwise stated.
The American Egg Board advises that eggs should not be
consumed raw. This book contains dishes made with raw or
lightly cooked eggs. It is prudent for more vulnerable people
such as pregnant and nursing mothers, invalids, the elderly,
babies, and young children to avoid uncooked or lightly cooked
dishes made with eggs. Once prepared, these dishes should
be kept refrigerated and used promptly.

Milk should be whole (full fat) unless otherwise stated.

Meat and poultry should be cooked thoroughly. To test if poultry
is cooked, pierce the flesh through the thickest part with a
skewer or fork—the juices should run clear, never pink or red.

Do not refreeze a dish that has been previously frozen.

Pepper should be freshly ground black pepper unless
otherwise stated.

Fresh herbs should be used, unless otherwise stated. If
unavailable, use dried herbs as an alternative but halve the
quantities stated.

Nuts and nut derivatives
This book includes dishes made with nuts and nut derivatives.
It is advisable for those with known allergic reactions to
nuts and nut derivatives and those who may be potentially
vulnerable to these allergies, such as pregnant and nursing
mothers, invalids, the elderly, babies, and children, to avoid
dishes made with nuts and nut oils. It is also prudent to check
the labels of preprepared ingredients for the possible inclusion
of nut derivatives.

Ovens should be preheated to the specified temperature—if
using a fan oven, follow the manufacturer's instructions for
adjusting the time and the temperature.

Contents

Introduction

Thai cooking has made a considerable impact on our own food in recent years. It has been a two-way process. Greatly increased numbers of visitors to Thailand—including backpackers, tourists, and Western business people—have been discovering for themselves the particular delights of Thailand's unique cuisine, and more and more Thais have been leaving home to set up restaurants all over the world, from Sydney to London, Auckland to San Francisco.

Whether at home or in countries far away, Thais always base their cooking on using fresh ingredients and remaining true to a typical Thai style: there is no compromising on authentic Thai recipes to suit the palates of the countries where their cooks happen to be.

Thailand's geographical position at the heart of South-east Asia means that its cooking has taken on and adapted to its own tastes the cuisines of countries around it, most notably China and India. European traders seeking spices and other goods also had some influence on Thai cooking: it was the Portuguese who introduced the chili to Thailand, which is today one of the most important ingredients in Thai cuisine. Not that there is just one kind of chili, of course, and about a dozen of the world's hottest varieties are widely grown in Thailand.

There are plenty of hot dishes—indeed some of them are very hot, and the Thais also make a great deal of use of the wok. Thai stir-fries, however, tend to be lighter and more highly spiced than Chinese ones and they are usually free of the cornstarch that is often used by the Chinese as a thickening agent.

Thai curries have a greater lightness of touch than those of India, allied to an aromatic sourness and a certain sweetness, which is uniquely Thai. The basic food of a Thai curry—pork, beef, chicken, or fish—is cut into more delicate slivers than the chunks which are usual in Indian cooking, and the fiery flavor comes from pastes—red curry paste based on red chilies and green curry paste on green ones. You will find recipes for both red and green curry pastes later in this introduction.

With the curry pastes are added fresh herbs, spices, and other flavorings which may include, depending on the flavor required, lemon grass, cilantro (the leaves, stems, and roots of fresh cilantro are all used in Thai cooking, as well as the seeds), lime leaves, three varieties of basil, galangal, ginger, garlic, and shallots. Thai curries get much of their creaminess from coconut milk and coconut cream, the recipe for which is also included in this introduction.

Another important element in Thai cooking is a fish sauce, called *nam pla* in Thailand, made from fermented fish and soy sauce. Pungent and salty, it replaces most or all of the salt which a Western cook would automatically add to a savory dish, and accentuates the flavors of the other ingredients. *Nam pla* is usually sold as Thai fish sauce in our supermarkets.

Rice or noodles provide the basic background or accompaniment for many Thai dishes, and you will find a whole chapter of rice and noodle recipes in this book. Thailand is, in fact, the world's largest rice-exporting country, producing a slightly sticky rice which is larger and softer than India's basmati rice. The main rice of Thailand is jasmine rice, or Thai fragrant rice—the name it is usually sold under in our supermarkets. If Thai fragrant rice is not available, any good quality long-grain rice, especially basmati, would suit the recipes here very well.

SOME BASIC RECIPES

At the heart of Thai cooking lies good stocks and those vitally important curry pastes mentioned previously. The selection of stocks and pastes here are ideal for using in the recipes in this book.

Chicken Stock

- 3½ lb boiling or other chicken
- 1 lb chicken giblets
- 1 onion, halved
- 1 carrot, roughly chopped
- 2 celery stalks, including leaves, roughly chopped
- 7 cups water
- 2 garlic cloves
- 1 lemon grass stalk, roughly chopped, or ¼ teaspoon grated lemon rind
- 10 black peppercorns
- 3 large red chilies

1 Put the chicken into a large, heavy-based saucepan or casserole dish with the giblets, onion, carrot, and celery and pour over cold water until the ingredients are just covered. Place over a very low heat, bring to a boil, as slowly as possible, and simmer for about *50 minutes*. When the liquid begins to simmer, remove the scum from the top until only white foam rises.

2 Add the remaining ingredients, cover the pan, and cook slowly for *2 hours*. Use a heat diffuser if you need to.

3 Remove the chicken and set aside for another use. Strain the stock without pressing the juices from the vegetables—this helps to keep it clear. You can use as much stock as you need immediately, and freeze the rest for future use.

Makes approx. 2 quarts

Fish Stock

- 1 lb raw white fish heads and bones, and shrimp heads and shells, if available
- 9 cups water
- 3 shallots
- 1 celery stalk, including leaves, roughly chopped
- ½ lemon grass stalk or ¼ teaspoon grated lemon rind
- 2 garlic cloves
- 2 tablespoons cilantro stems and roots

1 Put the fish trimmings and water into a large, heavy-based saucepan and bring to a boil. Skim off any scum.

2 Add the shallots, celery, lemon grass, garlic, and cilantro, cover the pan, and simmer for *50 minutes*.

3 Strain the stock and freeze the rest for future use.

Makes approx. 2½ quarts

Vegetable Stock

- 2 large onions, quartered
- 4 large red chilies
- 8 oz carrots, halved
- ¼ small white cabbage, halved
- 1 small head of celery, including leaves, chopped
- 1½ teaspoons chopped fresh cilantro leaves, stems, and roots
- 1 tablespoon basil leaves and stems
- ½ head of Chinese leaves, chopped
- ½ mooli or 6 radishes, peeled
- 25 black peppercorns
- ½ teaspoon salt
- 1 teaspoon palm sugar (jaggery) or light brown sugar
- 8 cups water

1 Put all the ingredients, including the water, into a heavy-based saucepan or casserole. Bring to a boil, cover, and simmer for *1 hour*.

2 Remove the lid and boil hard for *10 minutes*. Allow the stock to cool, then strain. Any stock you are not using immediately may be quickly cooled and frozen.

Makes approx. 2 quarts

Red Curry Paste

- 6 dried red chilies, seeded, soaked, and roughly chopped
- 2 tablespoons chopped lemon grass, or ¼ teaspoon grated lemon rind
- 1 teaspoon chopped cilantro roots or stems
- 1 tablespoon chopped shallots
- 1 tablespoon chopped garlic
- 1 teaspoon chopped galangal or fresh root ginger
- 2 teaspoons cilantro seeds
- 1 teaspoon cumin seeds
- 6 white peppercorns
- 1 teaspoon salt
- 1 teaspoon shrimp paste

1 Put all the ingredients in a blender or food processor and grind to a thick paste.

2 Alternatively, put the chilies in a mortar and crush them with a pestle, then add the lemon grass and crush it with the cilantro, and so on with all the other ingredients.

3 Transfer the paste to an airtight container—any that you do not use immediately may be stored in the refrigerator for up to 3 weeks.

GREEN CURRY PASTE

- 15 small green chilies
- 4 garlic cloves, halved
- 2 lemon grass stalks, finely chopped, or ¼ teaspoon grated lemon rind
- 2 lime leaves, torn
- 2 shallots, chopped
- 1 tablespoon chopped cilantro leaves, stems, and roots
- 1 inch piece of fresh root ginger, peeled and chopped
- 2 teaspoons cilantro seeds
- 1 teaspoon black peppercorns
- 1 teaspoon finely grated lime rind
- ½ teaspoon salt
- 2 tablespoons peanut oil

1 Put all the ingredients in a blender or food processor and grind to a thick paste.

2 Alternatively, put the chilies in a mortar and crush with a pestle, then add the garlic and crush it with the lemon grass, and so on with all the other ingredients, finally mixing in the oil with a spoon.

3 Transfer the paste to an airtight container—any that you do not use immediately may be stored in the refrigerator for up to 3 weeks.

COCONUT CREAM AND MILK
- 13 oz grated coconut
- 3¾ cups milk

1 Mix the coconut and milk together in a saucepan. Bring to a boil, then lower the heat, and simmer, stirring occasionally, until the mixture is reduced by one-third. Strain, pressing the mixture against the sides of the strainer to extract as much liquid as possible.

2 Pour the strained coconut milk into a bowl and chill in the refrigerator. When it is really cold, skim off the thicker "cream" that rises to the surface. The remaining liquid is the coconut milk.

GARLIC MIXTURE
- 2 tablespoons crushed garlic
- 2 tablespoons chopped cilantro roots or stems
- ½ tablespoon pepper

1 Put all the ingredients in a mortar and grind with a pestle until they are thoroughly blended and form a paste. If wished, the mixture can be made in advance and stored, covered, in the refrigerator for 1–2 days until required. This will enhance the flavor.

GARLIC OIL
- 4 tablespoons vegetable or sunflower oil
- 1 tablespoon crushed garlic

1 Heat the oil in a small frying pan and then add the crushed garlic. Cook slowly over a gentle heat until the garlic is golden, stirring occasionally. Use in recipes as required.

CRUSHED ROASTED NUTS
- 4 tablespoons unroasted peanuts or cashews

1 Dry-fry the nuts in a frying pan, without oil. Stir constantly until they turn golden in color. Remove from the heat and allow to cool.

2 Place the nuts in a plastic bag and break into small pieces using a rolling pin.

3 You can roast and crush a larger quantity of nuts, then store what you do not need for up to 1 month in an airtight container in the refrigerator.

USING BANANA LEAVES
Banana leaves are widely used in Thai cuisine as a way of both cooking and serving food. As well as adding a touch of the exotic to the presented meal, the leaf imparts a subtle flavor to

1 Warm the banana leaves and place some of the filling at one end of each leaf.

2 Fold one corner of the leaf over the filling, then the other. Repeat to form a neat triangular parcel.

3 Tie a loop of string around one corner of the triangle, then the other.

the dish, either acting as a kind of foil when wrapped around a filling and cooked, or used as a serving dish or container having been cut and shaped. The whole leaves can be bought, rolled, in packs of 4 or 5 from Thai or Oriental supermarkets and should be warmed over a flame or range top before using, to lighten the color and soften. Alternatively they can be dipped in boiling water.

SOME NOTES ABOUT CHILIES

Chilies are included in many of the recipes in this book and are used in amounts which ensure an authentic Thai taste. Quantities can be adjusted to suit personal taste: if you are unfamiliar with chilies, you may wish to start with relatively modest amounts, building up the heat as you become more used to them. Points to remember:

• Green chilies are hotter than the riper red chilies, although this may be something of an illusion, created by the fact that a chili, as it ripens, becomes sweeter and more rounded

in flavor, so the heat is less obvious.
• Among red chilies, smaller chilies tend to be hotter than larger, more elongated ones. The rounded Scotch bonnet and pointed bird's eye chilies pack powerful punches for their size.
• Among chilies usually available in supermarkets, the Fresno, which ranges in color from glossy green to orange and red, is medium-hot, and the jalapeño, although slightly smaller, is another hot one.
• Dried chilies are hotter than fresh ones: just 1 or 2 small dried red chilies or a small quantity of dried chili flakes will add a lot of heat to a recipe.
• Scraping the seeds from a chili will reduce its heat, since the seeds are the hottest part of a chili.
• Handle chilies with care, wearing gloves if your hands are sensitive, and be careful not to touch any part of your face, particularly your eyes, before you have washed your hands.

MENU PLANNING

Thai people love snacking, and stopping at a street market food stall several times a day to enjoy a freshly cooked and delicious snack is common. Meals at home and in restaurants are also taken in the same informal way. There are no distinct courses to a Thai meal, as there are in Western ones. Rather, a variety of dishes are presented at the same time, to provide a harmonious blend of flavors, textures, and cooking styles.

When planning a menu, keep the following points in mind and you will easily make memorable Thai meals:

• Soups are a very popular dish in Thailand. Often fiercely hot, they may be the only dish at a meal, especially in the middle of the day. It has become more usual for western Thai restaurants, especially in the West, to serve a soup as a starting course in a meal.
• A choice of two or three of the appetizers in this book make a very good light opening course for a Thai meal. Few Thais would object—after all, many of them buy their snacks two or three at a time from those popular street-vendors' stalls!
• For the main part of the meal, be careful to choose dishes that work well together. A fiery meat or poultry curry could overpower a very delicate fish dish, for instance. On the other hand, a fiery curry needs something cooling, like a simple rice dish or a salad.
• Do not serve dishes that have all been cooked in the same way: four stir fries together would tend to have the same texture. Instead, plan for a variety of cooking styles, such as a stir fry, a steamed dish, and, perhaps, something deep-fried.
• Similarly, try to vary the main ingredients, so that you have a meat dish, a fish dish, and a vegetable dish.
• Don't forget that rice and noodles provide the perfect accompaniment to more flavorful dishes. It is probably better to serve one or other of these at a meal, not both.
• Thais, like most Asians, are not great dessert eaters. If you do not want to serve one of the desserts in this book, then it is perfectly acceptable to serve a bowl of fresh fruits in season.

Soups and Snacks

Spicy soups and mouthwatering finger foods are Thai favorites, maintaining a wonderful balance of ingredients and textures. With soups that are thick and creamy or more like a consommé and crispy snacks which can be eaten on their own or accompanied by fiery sauces, this chapter has something for everyone, at any time of the day.

Mussel Soup

Preparation time: 30 minutes, plus soaking
Cooking time: 20 minutes

- 1 lb mussels
- ⅔ cup dried rice vermicelli
- 1¼ cups Coconut Milk (see page 8)
- 2½ cups Fish Stock (see page 7)
- 1 tablespoon finely chopped fresh root ginger
- 1 tablespoon chopped cilantro stems and roots
- ½ lemon grass stalk, chopped, or ¼ teaspoon grated lemon rind
- 2 small red chilies, finely sliced
- 1 tablespoon *nam pla* (fish sauce)
- 1 tablespoon lime juice
- 2 teapoons cilantro leaves, to garnish

1 Clean the mussels thoroughly, remove the beards, and leave to soak for about *1 hour* in cold water. Drain and tap any open shells to ensure that they close. If not, throw those mussels away. Soak the vermicelli in warm water for *15–20 minutes*.

2 Put the mussels into a saucepan, cover, and cook over a moderate heat for *3–4 minutes*. The mussels will open and release their liquid. Any that remain closed should be thrown away. Remove the mussels with a slotted spoon and reserve.

3 Add the remaining ingredients to the pan and simmer for *15 minutes*.

4 Finally, return the mussels to the pan and simmer for *1 minute*. Serve, garnished with cilantro leaves.

Serves 4

Chicken and Coconut Milk Soup

Preparation time: 6 minutes
Cooking time: 10 minutes

- 2½ cups Chicken Stock (see page 7)
- 6 kaffir lime leaves, torn, or ¼ teaspoon grated lime rind
- 1 lemon grass stalk, sliced diagonally, or ¼ teaspoon grated lemon rind
- 2-inch piece of galangal or fresh root ginger, peeled and finely sliced
- 1 cup Coconut Milk (see page 8)
- 8 tablespoons *nam pla* (fish sauce)
- 2 teaspoons palm sugar (jaggery) or light brown sugar
- 6 tablespoons lime juice
- 8 oz chicken, skinned and cut into small pieces
- 4 tablespoons chili oil or 4 small chilies, finely sliced (optional)

1 Heat the stock and add the lime leaves, lemon grass, and galangal. Stir them in and, as the stock is simmering, add the coconut milk, *nam pla*, sugar, and lime juice. Stir well, then add the chicken pieces and simmer for *5 minutes*.

2 Just before serving, add the chili oil or chilies, if you like, stir again and serve.

Serves 4

Shrimp and Lime Soup

Preparation time: 10–15 minutes
Cooking time: 20 minutes

- 1½ lb raw shrimp
- 8 cups water
- 6 small kaffir lime leaves, or ¼ teaspoon grated lime rind
- 1 tablespoon chopped lemon grass, or ¼ teaspoon grated lemon rind
- 2 teaspoons *nam pla* (fish sauce)
- ⅓ cup lime juice
- 4 tablespoons cilantro leaves, chopped
- 3 tablespoons sliced green onions (scallions)
- 1 red chili, seeded and sliced into 1-inch strips
- salt and pepper
- slivers of green onion (scallion), to garnish

1 Peel the shrimp and remove the dark vein running along the back. Wash them under cold running water, drain, and pat dry with paper towels. Set aside while you make the soup.

2 Pour the water into a large saucepan and bring to a boil. Add the lime leaves and lemon grass, reduce the heat, and simmer for *10 minutes*. Add the *nam pla* and cook for a further *5 minutes*.

3 Add the shrimp and lime juice to the pan and cook gently over a very low heat for a few minutes, until the shrimp become firm and turn a pale pink color.

4 Add the chopped cilantro leaves, green onions, and red chili strips to the soup. Check the seasoning, adding salt and pepper if wished, and serve very hot in individual bowls, garnished with slivers of green onion.

Serves 6

Rice Noodle Soup

Preparation time: 10 minutes, plus soaking
Cooking time: 8 minutes

- 3 cups Vegetable Stock
  (see page 7)
- 3 green onions (scallions),
  cut into 1-inch lengths
- 2 baby corn cobs, sliced
  diagonally
- 1 tomato, finely diced
- 1 red onion, cut into fine
  slivers
- 6 kaffir lime leaves, or
  ¼ teaspoon grated lime rind
- 1 celery stalk, chopped

- 4 oz fried tofu, diced
- 1 tablespoon soy sauce
- 1 teaspoon pepper
- 1 teaspoon crushed dried
  chilies
- 6 oz flat (wide) rice noodles,
  soaked and drained
- fresh cilantro sprigs, to
  garnish
- lime quarters, to serve

1 Heat the stock in a saucepan and add all of the ingredients except the noodles and a few of the red onion slivers.

2 Bring to a boil for *30 seconds*, then lower the heat to a simmer and cook for *5 minutes*.

3 Add the noodles and simmer for another *2 minutes*.

4 Pour into a serving bowl, garnish with cilantro sprigs and the remaining red onion slivers, and serve with lime quarters.

Serves 4

Banana and Chili Soup

Preparation time: 15 minutes
Cooking time: 8 minutes

- 1 tablespoon peanut oil
- 2 green onions (scallions), including green shoots, sliced
- 4 garlic cloves, sliced
- 1 cup Coconut Milk (see page 8)
- 1¾ cups Vegetable Stock (see page 7)
- ¼ teaspoon ground white pepper

- 3 teaspoons *nam pla* (fish sauce) or soy sauce
- ¼ teaspoon salt
- ½ teaspoon sugar
- 1 large banana, peeled and cut diagonally into thin slices
- 1 large red chili, sliced diagonally
- green onion (scallion) strips, to garnish

1 Heat the oil in a saucepan and quickly fry the green onion and garlic for about *30 seconds*. Add all the other ingredients except the banana and chili slices, and cook for *5 minutes*.

2 Pour the soup into a blender or food processor, add about three-quarters of the banana and chili slices, and purée until smooth. Return the mixture to the pan, add the remaining banana and chili slices, and warm through for *3 minutes*.

3 Serve hot, garnished with green onion strips, made into curls, if liked.

Serves 4

Pumpkin Soup

Preparation time: 30 minutes
Cooking time: 15 minutes

- 1 teaspoon finely sliced lemon grass, or ¼ teaspoon grated lemon rind
- 1 teaspoon peeled and finely sliced galangal or root ginger
- 1 tablespoon basil leaves
- ½ green bell pepper, chopped
- 3 kaffir lime leaves, or ¼ teaspoon grated lime rind
- ½ cup water
- 1 tablespoon peanut oil
- 2 garlic cloves, finely chopped
- 10 shallots, peeled and thinly sliced
- 1 teaspoon crushed dried chilies
- 1 small red chili, chopped
- 2 cups Vegetable Stock (see page 7)
- ½ cup green beans, chopped
- 3 tablespoons *nam pla* (fish sauce) or soy sauce
- 1½ lb pumpkin, peeled and cubed
- 1 teaspoon sugar
- 1 teaspoon ground white pepper
- 1 tablespoon Crushed Roasted Nuts (see page 8) or crunchy peanut butter
- 3 teaspoons curry powder
- ¾ cup Coconut Milk (see page 8)
- 2 teaspoons cornstarch
- basil leaves, to garnish

1 Blend the lemon grass, galangal, basil, green bell pepper, lime leaves, and water in a blender or food processor, then strain and throw away the liquid, reserving the purée.

2 Heat the oil in a large saucepan. Add the garlic, shallots, and dried and fresh chilies and stir-fry over a high heat for *1 minute*.

3 Add the purée, four-fifths of the stock, the green beans, *nam pla,* and pumpkin. Stir over a moderate heat. Add the sugar, pepper, nuts, and curry powder and stir again. When the pumpkin is tender, after about *10 minutes*, add the coconut milk and bring to a hard boil for *1 minute*.

4 Blend the remaining stock with the cornstarch until it is smooth, add to the soup, and stir to thicken.

5 Ladle the soup into a large serving bowl and place the basil on top, to garnish.

Serves 4

Clear Bean Curd Soup

Bean curd is ideal for use in soups because it takes on the other flavors of the dish. It is also known as tofu, which is its Japanese name.

Preparation time: 10 minutes
Cooking time: 10 minutes

- 4 cups Vegetable Stock (see page 7)
- 8 oz ground pork
- 10 oz bean curd, cut into large squares
- 2 cups fresh bean sprouts, trimmed
- 4 tablespoons *nam pla* (fish sauce)
- 2 green onions (scallions), finely chopped
- 1 celery stalk with leaves, chopped
- pepper, to taste

1 Heat the stock in a saucepan, then place the ground pork in a bowl. Add about a cup of the hot stock and stir with a fork to break up the meat so that no lumps remain.

2 Add the pork mixture to the stock in the saucepan and cook over a moderate heat for *5 minutes*. Stir in the bean curd, bean sprouts, *nam pla*, green onions, and celery and bring to the boil. Lower the heat and simmer for a further *3 minutes*.

3 Transfer to a serving bowl, season with pepper, and serve on its own as an appetizer, or as an accompaniment to the main meal, in the traditional Thai way.

Serves 4

Egg Rolls

Preparation time: 25 minutes
Cooking time: 20–25 minutes

- 8 oz egg roll wrappers, each 5 inches square
- 1 egg, beaten
- oil, for deep-frying

FILLING:
- 2 tablespoons vegetable oil
- 2 tablespoons Garlic Mixture (see page 8)
- 4 oz crabmeat
- 4 oz raw shrimp, shelled and finely chopped
- 4 oz ground pork
- 4 oz dried rice vermicelli, soaked and cut into ½-inch lengths

- 4 oz mushrooms, chopped
- 2 tablespoons *nam pla* (fish sauce)
- 2 tablespoons light soy sauce
- 1 teaspoon sugar
- 5 green onions (scallions), finely chopped

TO GARNISH:
- 1 large red chili, cut into fine julienne strips
- 1 lime, sliced
- basil leaves

1 To make the filling, heat the oil in a wok or large, deep frying pan. Add the garlic mixture and stir-fry for *1 minute* until golden brown. Add the crabmeat, shrimp, and pork and stir-fry for *10–12 minutes*, or until lightly cooked. Add the vermicelli, mushrooms, *nam pla*, soy sauce, sugar, and green onions and stir-fry for a further *5 minutes* until all the liquid has been absorbed. Set aside to cool.

2 Separate the egg roll wrappers and spread them out under a clean dish towel to keep them soft. Put about 2 tablespoons of the filling on each egg roll wrapper, and brush the left and right borders with beaten egg.

3 Fold the sides over the filling and then roll up like a sausage. Brush the top edge with more beaten egg and then seal. Keep the filled rolls covered while you make the remaining egg rolls in the same way.

4 Heat the oil in a wok or heavy-based pan and cook the egg rolls, a few at a time, for *5–8 minutes*, or until golden brown. Turn once during cooking so that they brown evenly. Drain on paper towels and serve hot, garnished with strips of red chili, slices of lime, and a few basil leaves.

Serves 6

variation _____

Vegetarian Egg Rolls

Preparation time: 25 minutes
Cooking time: about 10 minutes

1 Heat 1 tablespoon peanut oil in a wok or large, deep frying pan. Add 2 cloves finely chopped garlic, 1 cup bean sprouts, 1 cup shredded white cabbage, 2–3 tablespoons shredded fresh shiitake mushrooms, and ⅓ cup of finely chopped celery. Stir-fry for *30 seconds*, then add 1 teaspoon sugar, 2 teaspoons soy sauce, and 2 oz dried cellophane noodles, soaked, drained, and cut into short lengths with scissors. Stir-fry for *1 minute*, then remove from the heat and set aside to cool. Continue from step 2 in the main recipe.

Fried Wonton

Preparation time: 15 minutes
Cooking time: 20 minutes

- 8 oz ground pork
- 1 tablespoon finely chopped
  onions
- 2 teaspoons Garlic Mixture
  (see page 8)
- ½ tablespoon *nam pla* (fish
  sauce)
- 20 wonton wrappers
  (suitable for frying)

- 1 egg yolk, beaten
- oil, for deep-frying
- Chili Sauce (right) or Plum
  Sauce (see page 28), to serve
- 1 green onion (scallion), cut
  into very fine slivers, to
  garnish

1 Put the ground pork in a small bowl with the chopped onions, garlic mixture, and *nam pla*. Mix well together to combine all the ingredients to a thick paste.

2 Spread the wonton wrappers out on a work surface and put a teaspoon of the pork mixture into the center of each wrapper.

3 Brush the edges of the wrappers with the egg yolk, and then fold the wrappers over to enclose the filling and make a triangular shape. Press the edges firmly together, sealing with more egg yolk if necessary.

4 Heat the oil in a wok or large, heavy-based frying pan and fry the filled wontons, a few at a time, for about *5 minutes*, until they are golden brown. Turn them over in the oil if necessary to brown both sides. Drain on paper towels and serve hot with chili sauce or plum sauce, garnished with very fine slivers of green onion.

Serves 4–5

Chili Sauce

Preparation time: 3–4 minutes
Cooking time: 10–15 minutes

- 8 fresh red chilies, chopped
- 4 garlic cloves, crushed
- 1 tablespoon *nam pla* (fish
  sauce)
- 2 teaspoons sugar

- 2 tablespoons lime or lemon
  juice
- ¼ teaspoon salt
- ½ cup water
- 2 tablespoons peanut oil

1 Put the chilies, garlic, *nam pla*, sugar, lime or lemon juice, and the salt in a small saucepan. Stir in the water and oil. Bring to a boil, reduce the heat, and simmer gently for *10–15 minutes*. Blend until smooth in a food processor or blender. Store in a screwtop jar in the refrigerator for a maximum of 2 weeks. Use as required.

Steamed Wonton

Preparation time: 15 minutes
Cooking time: 30 minutes

- 16 wonton wrappers
- oil, for drizzling
FILLING:
- 6 raw shrimp, shelled
- 4 oz ground pork
- ⅓ cup chopped onions
- 2 garlic cloves
- 5 water chestnuts
- 1 teaspoon palm sugar (jaggery) or light brown sugar
- 1 tablespoon light soy sauce
- 1 egg
- Soy and Vinegar Dipping Sauce (right) or Hot Sweet Sauce (see page 24), to serve

1 To make the filling, blend all the ingredients in a blender or food processor.

2 Put 1 heaping teaspoonful of the filling into the center of a wrapper, placed over your thumb and index finger. As you push the filled wrapper down through the circle your fingers form, tighten the top, shaping it but leaving the top open. Repeat this process with all of the wrappers.

3 Put the filled wontons onto a plate and place the plate in a steamer. Drizzle a little oil on top of the wontons, put the lid on, and steam for *30 minutes*.

4 Serve the wontons hot or warm, with the dipping sauces served separately in bowls.

Serves 4

Soy and Vinegar Dipping Sauce

Preparation time: 2 minutes

- 3 tablespoons distilled white vinegar or Chinese rice vinegar
- 3 tablespoons dark soy sauce
- 1½ teaspoons superfine sugar
- 2 small red chilies, finely sliced

1 Combine all the ingredients in a bowl and stir until the sugar has dissolved.

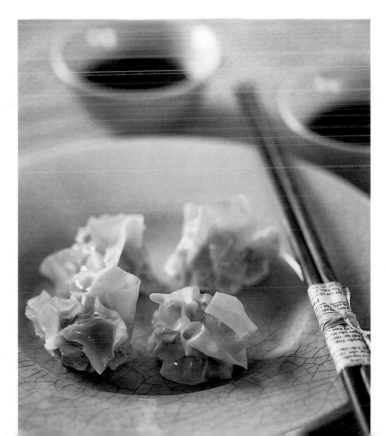

Crispy Wrapped Shrimp

Preparation time: 20 minutes
Cooking time: 5 minutes

- 3 oz ground pork
- 4 raw shrimp, shelled and
  minced
- ½ teaspoon sugar
- ¼ cup finely chopped onions
- 1 garlic clove, finely chopped
- 2 teaspoons light soy sauce
- 12 raw shrimp

- 12 egg roll wrappers
- 1 egg white, beaten
- oil, for deep-frying
- basil or cilantro sprig, to
  garnish (optional)
- Hot Sweet Sauce (right),
  to serve

1 Mix the ground pork, 4 minced raw shrimp, sugar, onions, garlic, and soy sauce together in a bowl and set aside.

2 Shell the other 12 shrimp, leaving the tails intact, and carefully cut them open, making sure you do not cut right through them. Keep the shell-on tails uncut.

3 Put 1 teaspoon or more of the ground mixture onto each opened shrimp. Take an egg roll wrapper and pull one corner about three-quarters of the way towards the opposite corner. Place a shrimp onto the double thickness of wrapper, leaving the tail free, and roll it up, tucking the ends in and sticking it down with a little bit of egg white. Continue until all the shrimp are wrapped.

4 Heat the oil in a wok and deep-fry the shrimp rolls until golden—this should take about *5 minutes*. Remove from the wok and drain on paper towels.

5 Garnish with basil or cilantro, if using, and serve with hot sweet sauce.

Makes 12

Hot Sweet Sauce

Preparation time: 1 minute
Cooking time: 1–2 minutes

- ½ cup distilled white vinegar
  or Chinese rice vinegar
- ⅓ cup palm sugar (jaggery) or
  light brown sugar
- ¼ teaspoon salt

- 1 small green chili, finely
  chopped
- 1 small red chili, finely
  chopped

1 Pour the vinegar into a small saucepan and place over a gentle heat. Add the sugar and salt and cook, stirring, until the sugar has dissolved. Remove from the heat and allow to cool.

2 Pour the cooled sauce into a small bowl and add all of the chopped chilies.

Stuffed Green Peppers

For this recipe it is best to use long green peppers rather than the squat bell variety. The peppers should be about 8 inches long and ¾–1 inch wide at their fattest part. If you like, you can prepare the stuffing and fill the peppers in advance, then coat them in batter and deep-fry them at the last minute.

Preparation time: 25 minutes
Cooking time: 12–14 minutes

- 8 large, mild green peppers or 4 bell peppers
- peanut oil, for deep-frying
- chives, to garnish

FILLING:
- 3 baby corn cobs, roughly chopped
- 3 garlic cloves, halved
- 4 tablespoons peanut oil
- ½ cup finely chopped onions
- 1 tomato, diced
- 2 fresh shiitake or chestnut mushrooms, finely sliced

- ½ cup green beans, finely sliced
- ½ teaspoon sugar
- 1 tablespoon soy sauce
- ¼ teaspoon salt
- 1 teaspoon pepper
- 2 eggs

BATTER:
- 3 tablespoons cornstarch
- ¼ cup water
- ½ teaspoon salt
- ¼ teaspoon pepper

1 Remove the ends from the green peppers and cut out the seeds. Set the hollow peppers aside.

2 To make the filling, quickly blend the corn and garlic in a blender or food processor.

3 Heat 3 tablespoons of the oil in a wok or frying pan and cook the onions for *30 seconds*. Add the tomato and mushrooms and cook, stirring, for *1 minute*. Add the green beans and cook for *30 seconds* before adding the corn and garlic mixture, the sugar, soy sauce, salt, and pepper. At this point you may need to add the remaining oil. Break the eggs into the mixture and stir well. Cook for *2 minutes*, remove from the heat, and turn the mixture out onto a plate.

4 Stuff the peppers with the filling, as full as you can.

5 Mix the batter ingredients together thoroughly in a bowl.

6 Heat the oil for deep-frying in a wok. Coat half of the peppers in the batter, place them in the hot oil, and cook them for *6–7 minutes*, moving them around gently until they are golden on all sides. Remove the peppers from the oil with a slotted spoon and drain on paper towels. Repeat with the remaining peppers and batter.

7 Arrange the cooked peppers on a plate, garnish with chives, and serve immediately.

Makes 8

Thai Egg Strips

Preparation time: 5 minutes
Cooking time: 2–3 minutes

- 3 eggs, beaten
- 1 shallot, finely sliced
- green shoots of 1 green onion (scallion), sliced
- 1–2 small red chilies, finely chopped

- 1 tablespoon chopped fresh cilantro leaves
- 1 tablespoon peanut oil
- salt and pepper
- julienne strips of green onion (scallion), to garnish (optional)

1 Mix all the ingredients, except the oil, in a bowl. Season to taste with salt and pepper.

2 Heat the oil in a frying pan or wok, pour in the egg mixture, and swirl it around the pan to produce a large, thin omelet. Cook for *1–2 minutes* until firm.

3 Slide the omelet out onto a plate and roll it up as though it were a pancake. Allow to cool.

4 When the omelet is cool, cut the roll crossways into ¼-inch or ½-inch sections, depending on how wide you want your strips to be. Serve them rolled up or straightened out, in a heap. Garnish with strips of green onion, if wished.

Serves 2

Fried Golden Bags

Preparation time: 25 minutes
Cooking time: 5–10 minutes

- 20 wonton wrappers
  (suitable for frying)
- 20 fresh flowering chives,
  about 4 inches long, plus
  extra for garnishing
- oil, for deep-frying

FILLING:

- ½ cup canned water
  chestnuts, chopped
- 8 oz crabmeat
- 2 oz raw shrimp, shelled and
  chopped

- 2 teaspoons Garlic Mixture
  (see page 8)
- 2 green onions (scallions),
  chopped
- 1 green chili, seeded and
  chopped
- 1 tablespoon dark soy sauce
- 1 tablespoon *nam pla* (fish
  sauce)
- Plum Sauce (right), or Chili
  Sauce (see page 22), to serve

1 To make the filling, put all the ingredients in a large mixing bowl and mix together until thoroughly combined. You should end up with a thick paste.

2 Spread the wonton wrappers out on a flat surface and divide the crabmeat filling equally between them, putting a spoonful into the center of each wrapper. Pull the 4 corners up into the middle to make little bags.

3 Secure the little bags around the middle where the corners of the wonton wrappers are gathered together with the chives. Take care that the chives do not break as you tie them.

4 Heat the oil for deep-frying in a wok or deep-fat fryer. Fry the little bags in batches, a few at a time, for *2–3 minutes* until they are crisp and golden brown. Remove and drain on paper towels. Serve very hot with either plum sauce or chili sauce, garnished with a few of the chives.

Serves 4–5

Plum Sauce

Preparation time: 5 minutes
Cooking time: 17–18 minutes

- 3 preserved plums (available
  from Asian stores), plus
  1 tablespoon liquid from the jar
- ⅔ cup water
- 6 tablespoons superfine
  sugar

1 Put the plums, the plum liquid, and water in a saucepan and mix well together. Bring to a boil and allow to boil for *1–2 minutes*, stirring constantly with a wooden spoon to break up the plums.

2 Press the mixture through a sieve and strain into the pan. Add the sugar, stirring well until dissolved, and bring back to a boil. Reduce the heat and simmer for *15 minutes*, or until the sauce thickens and turns reddish in color. When cool, pour into a screwtop jar and store in the refrigerator.

variation
Vegetarian Golden Bags

Preparation time: 25 minutes
Cooking time: 5 minutes

1 To make a vegetarian filling; heat 2 tablespoons peanut oil in a wok or deep frying pan, add 2 chopped garlic cloves, 3 finely sliced baby corn cobs, 5 finely chopped fresh shiitake mushrooms, ¼ cup very finely sliced green beans, and ⅛ cup finely chopped onions. Stir-fry for *1–2 minutes*. Push the vegetables to the side of the wok, pour in 1 tablespoon peanut oil, and break an egg in to it. Break the yolk, stir it, and mix in the vegetables for about *1 minute*. Add ½ teaspoon sugar, 1 tablespoon soy sauce, and season with salt and pepper to taste. Mix well. Remove from the heat and leave to cool. Continue with step 2 of the main recipe.

Vegetables and Salads

This chapter includes a selection of typically Thai salad and vegetable dishes, suitable for both main courses and accompaniments. They are served with delicious spicy dressings and, like all Thai recipes, are simple to make. And, as the dishes are low in fat, they are good for you too.

Stir-fried Vegetables with Cashews

Preparation time: 20 minutes
Cooking time: 2–3 minutes

- 2 cups Chinese leaves, chopped into 1-inch pieces
- 1 cup cauliflower florets
- 1 cup broccoli, separated into florets
- 1 cup white cabbage, chopped
- 2 baby corn cobs, sliced diagonally
- 1 tomato, cut into 8 pieces
- 5 garlic cloves, chopped
- ⅓ cup cashews, roasted (see page 8)
- 1½ tablespoons soy sauce
- 1 teaspoon sugar
- ½ cup water
- 2½ tablespoons peanut oil
- pepper

1 Mix all the ingredients, except the oil, in a bowl. Season with pepper, to taste.

2 Heat a wok or deep frying pan and add the oil. Tip in the contents of the bowl and cook over a high heat, stirring and turning, for *2–3 minutes*. Taste and season with pepper, if necessary. Serve at once.

Serves 3–4

Vegetables with Oyster Sauce

Preparation time: 15 minutes
Cooking time: 6–7 minutes

- 3 tablespoons vegetable oil
- 1 garlic clove, crushed
- 2 cups cabbage, shredded
- 2 cups cauliflower florets
- ½ teaspoon pepper
- 2 tablespoons oyster sauce
- ¾ cup Chicken or Vegetable
  Stock (see page 7)

- 2 cups broccoli, separated
  into florets
- 2 carrots, cut into fine strips
- 2 cups mushrooms, thinly
  sliced
- 1 onion, sliced into rings
- 1 cup bean sprouts
- shredded carrot, to garnish
- boiled white rice, to serve

1 Heat the oil in a wok or deep frying pan. Add the crushed garlic, and then stir-fry quickly over a medium heat until golden. Do not allow it to get too brown.

2 Add the shredded cabbage and cauliflower florets and season with the pepper. Stir in the oyster sauce and the stock, and then cook, stirring constantly, for *3 minutes*.

3 Add the broccoli, carrots, mushrooms, onion, and bean sprouts to the wok. Stir fry for *2 minutes*. Transfer the fried vegetables to a large warm dish or platter, garnish with shredded carrot, and serve immediately with rice.

Serves 4

Curried Vegetable Salad

Preparation time: 25 minutes
Cooking time: 4–6 minutes

- 2 celery stalks, roughly chopped
- 4 carrots, thinly sliced
- 2 cups cabbage, finely sliced
- 1 cup thin green beans
- ½ red bell pepper, diced
- ½ green bell pepper, diced
- 4 cups bean sprouts
- 1 cup canned water chestnuts, drained and sliced

CURRY DRESSING:
- ½ cup creamed coconut
- ⅔ cup water
- 2 tablespoons peanut oil

- 2 tablespoons Red Curry Paste (see page 7)
- 2 tablespoons dark soy sauce
- 2 tablespoons lime juice
- 2 teaspoons palm sugar (jaggery) or light brown sugar
- ¼ teaspoon salt
- 1 teaspoon ground cilantro
- 2 teaspoons ground cumin
- 3 tablespoons Crushed Roasted Nuts (see page 8)

TO GARNISH:
- coconut slivers
- mint sprigs (optional)

1 Bring a large saucepan of water to a boil and plunge in all the vegetables, except the bean sprouts and water chestnuts. Blanch them by boiling for *3–4 minutes*. They should retain their fresh color and be slightly tender but still crisp. Drain and mix in a bowl with the bean sprouts and water chestnuts.

2 To make the curry dressing, put the creamed coconut in a bowl and cover with the water. Stir well until the creamed coconut has completely dissolved, and set aside.

3 Heat the peanut oil in a small wok or frying pan. Add the red curry paste to the pan and stir well over a low heat for *1–2 minutes*. Add the creamed coconut, soy sauce, lime juice, sugar, salt, cilantro, cumin, and nuts. Stir well and heat through gently for *3–4 minutes*. Pour the dressing over the vegetables and toss gently. Transfer to a serving dish and serve warm, garnished with coconut slivers and mint sprigs, if using.

Serves 4–6

Thai Basics

Fundamental to the success of any Thai dish are the ingredients which provide its unique taste and texture. Asian ingredients are becoming a common sight in most supermarkets, and having to hand this selection of basics will ensure that you maintain a wonderful balance of Thai flavors every time.

Flat rice noodles

Mixed pickled chilies

Coconut

Lemon grass

Tamarind paste

Coconut is used as a cream or milk (see page 8) to add texture and flavor to spicy curries, and as a sweet ingredient for desserts.
Lemon grass is an aromatic tropical grass, also available dried or as a powder, which adds a subtle lemon aroma and flavor to soups, salads, and curries. Use grated lemon rind as an alternative.
Tamarind paste is made from the ground pulp of the tamarind tree pod. With a sharp but fruity taste, it is often used as a souring agent for curries and soups. Use lemon juice as a substitute.
Flat (wide) rice noodles are ribbon-like white noodles made from rice flour and may be bought fresh or dried.
Mixed pickled chilies are ideal for cooking—a jar will keep in the fridge for months. The chilies are generally a mixture of hot to very hot varieties, so use with caution.
Salted peanuts are usually roasted and crushed, then combined with spicy meat or

Green curry paste

Wonton wrappers

Nam pla

Salted peanuts

Red curry paste

Rice vermicelli

Egg noodles (dried)

vegetable curries, or ground to a paste to make a sauce to accompany satay dishes. **Rice vermicelli** are white, thin thread-like noodles often sold dried in long bundles. They may be deep-fried or soaked in water and then boiled.

Wonton wrappers are noodle dough squares made from eggs and flour, available fresh or frozen. Use to create miniature parcels with a filling. **Green and Red curry pastes** are hot pastes made from the respective colored

chilies plus a mixture of herbs and spices (see pages 7 and 8), and form the basis for many Thai curries. **Nam pla** is made from fermented fish, salt, and soy sauce and provides flavoring to a variety of fish and noodle

dishes. May also be used as a general seasoning. **Egg noodles (dried)** are essential to Thai cuisine, either as a whole meal or as an accompaniment. Available either flat or as threads, they may also be bought fresh.

Chicken and Papaya Salad

Papaya is often cooked or served with poultry or meat in Thailand as a cooling contrast to a spicy dressing. If papayas are difficult to obtain, mango, pineapple, or melon can be substituted

Preparation time: 30 minutes
Cooking time: 15 minutes

DRESSING:

- 2 small green or red chilies, seeded and chopped
- 2 large garlic cloves, chopped
- finely grated rind of 1 lime
- 6 tablespoons lime juice
- 2–3 tablespoons *nam pla* (fish sauce)
- 2–3 tablespoons palm sugar (jaggery) or light brown sugar, to taste

SALAD:

- 2 ripe papayas
- 1 crisp lettuce, e.g. iceberg, leaves separated
- ½ large cucumber, thinly sliced
- 1½ cups bean sprouts
- 1 lb chicken breast fillets, skinned
- corn or peanut oil, for brushing

1 First make the dressing. Put the chilies, garlic, and lime rind in a mortar and pound with a pestle until crushed to a paste.

2 Stir in the lime juice and *nam pla* until evenly mixed with the chili and garlic paste, then add some sugar to taste. Cover and set aside while preparing the salad ingredients and cooking the chicken.

3 Peel the papayas, cut each one in half lengthways, and scoop out and discard the seeds. Slice the flesh thinly.

4 Arrange the lettuce leaves around the edge of a serving dish, then place the papaya, cucumber, and bean sprouts attractively on top.

5 Brush the chicken breasts liberally with oil. Cook under a preheated hot broiler for about *7 minutes* on each side, until cooked through.

6 Place the chicken on a board. With a very sharp knife, cut it into bite-sized diagonal slices. Arrange the chicken on top of the salad and sprinkle over the dressing. Let the salad stand for a few minutes before serving.

Serves 4

Duck Salad

Preparation time: 8–10 minutes
Cooking time: 3 minutes

- ¼ roast duck
- 6 small green chilies, finely
  sliced
- ½ red onion, finely sliced
- 1½ teaspoons fresh cilantro
  leaf, stem, and root, finely
  chopped
- ½ tomato, cut into quarters
- 4 tablespoons lime juice
- 1 teaspoon palm sugar
  (jaggery) or light brown sugar

- 1½ tablespoons *nam pla*
  (fish sauce)

TO SERVE:
- lettuce leaves
- mint leaves

TO GARNISH:
- grated carrot
- shredded white cabbage

1 Remove the skin and meat from the duck and cut it into small pieces.

2 Heat a wok and then turn the heat off. Put the duck into the wok to warm it through, and then add all the remaining ingredients, stirring and turning them thoroughly for about *3 minutes*.

3 To serve, arrange the lettuce leaves and mint on one side of a serving dish and place the duck salad beside them. Garnish with grated carrot and shredded white cabbage.

Serves 3–4

Garlic Chicken Salad

Preparation time: 15 minutes
Cooking time: 20 minutes

- 4 boneless, skinless chicken breasts
- Garlic Oil, for brushing (see page 8)
- crisp lettuce leaves
- 5 green onions (scallions), chopped
- ½ cucumber, diced
- 1 cup oyster mushrooms, thinly sliced
- ½ cup canned water chestnuts, drained and sliced

DRESSING:
- 3 tablespoons *nam pla* (fish sauce)
- 4 tablespoons lime juice
- 1 garlic clove, crushed
- 2 teaspoons palm sugar (jaggery) or light brown sugar
- 2 red chilies, seeded and cut into shreds

TO GARNISH:
- 1 tablespoon chopped fresh cilantro
- red and green chilies, sliced

1 Place the chicken breasts on a broiler pan and brush with garlic oil. Cook under a preheated hot broiler for about *7 minutes* on each side, until cooked through and golden brown. Set the chicken aside to cool while you prepare the salad.

2 Arrange the lettuce leaves in a serving dish and sprinkle with the chopped green onions, diced cucumber, sliced oyster mushrooms, and water chestnuts.

3 To make the dressing, put the *nam pla*, lime juice, garlic, sugar, and shredded red chilies in a small saucepan. Place the pan over a low heat and cook very gently, stirring all the time, until the sugar has dissolved. Remove from the heat.

4 Cut the cooked chicken breasts into strips and arrange them on top of the salad. Cover with the warm dressing, and then garnish with chopped cilantro and sliced red and green chilies. Serve the salad warm.

Serves 4

variation
Garlic Duck Salad

Preparation time: 15 minutes
Cooking time: 20 minutes

1 Substitute 4 boneless duck breasts for the chicken breasts. Follow the main recipe, but be sure to broil the duck until the skin is crisp and golden. Alternatively, cook the duck in a range-top grill pan until crisp and cooked completely through.

Sweet and Sour Salad

Preparation time: 15 minutes

- 1 large garlic clove, chopped
- 2 small Thai chilies, chopped, or ½ teaspoon ground chili
- ½ cup carrots, thinly sliced
- 2 cups white cabbage, thinly sliced
- 2 green beans, cut into 1-inch lengths
- 2 tomatoes, chopped
- 1½ tablespoons *nam pla* (fish sauce)
- 3 tablespoons lemon juice
- 3 tablespoons sugar
- 1 tablespoon ground dried shrimp
- 2 tablespoons Crushed Roasted Nuts (see page 8)
- basil leaves, to garnish
- 1 frisée lettuce, separated into leaves, to serve

1 Grind the garlic and chilies to a paste in a blender or food processor. Alternatively, pound them using a pestle and mortar. Transfer the mixture to a bowl, add the carrots, cabbage, green beans, tomatoes, *nam pla*, lemon juice, sugar, ground dried shrimp, and nuts and mix well so that all the ingredients are thoroughly blended.

2 Arrange a bed of lettuce in a shallow serving dish, top with the salad, garnish with basil leaves, and serve.

Serves 4

Green Mango Salad

Preparation time: 12 minutes

- 1 large, hard green mango,
  peeled and grated
- 1 red onion, chopped
- 1 tablespoon palm sugar
  (jaggery) or light brown sugar
- 1 tablespoon lime juice
- 1 tablespoon soy sauce
- ⅛ teaspoon salt

- 1 teaspoon crushed dried
  chilies
- ½ cup Crushed Roasted Nuts
  (see page 8)

TO GARNISH:

- fresh cilantro leaves
- 1 red chili, roughly chopped
- red onion slivers

1 Stir the mango and red onion together in a large bowl. Add the sugar, lime juice, soy sauce, salt, and chilies and stir thoroughly for *1–2 minutes*.

2 Add the nuts, give the salad a final stir, and turn out on to a serving dish.

3 Garnish the salad with cilantro leaves, chopped chili, and red onion slivers before serving.

Serves 3–4

Meat and Poultry

Meat and poultry dishes from Thailand cover a sensationally spicy range of tastes, from rich exotic curries of Indian influence to tangy stir-fries and subtle herb marinades. With wonderfully simple recipes and the uniquely Thai use of fish, citrus, and coconut flavors, this chapter brings a fresh approach to cooking with duck, chicken, beef, and pork.

Red Curry Duck

Preparation time: 12–15 minutes
Cooking time: 5 minutes

- ¼ **roast duck**
- **1 tablespoon oil**
- **1½ tablespoons Red Curry Paste (see page 7)**
- **⅔ cup Coconut Milk (see page 8)**
- **1 tablespoon palm sugar (jaggery) or light brown sugar**
- **3 kaffir lime leaves, torn, or ¼ teaspoon grated lime rind**
- **½ cup peas (fresh or frozen)**
- **1 large red chili, sliced diagonally**

- **4 tablespoons Chicken Stock (see page 7)**
- **2 tomatoes, finely diced**
- **⅔ cup fresh or canned pineapple, cut into chunks, plus extra to serve (optional)**
- **1 tablespoon *nam pla* (fish sauce)**
- **noodles, to serve (optional)**

TO GARNISH:
- **red pepper strips**
- **green onion (scallion) strips**

1 Take the skin and meat off the duck, chop it into bite-sized pieces, and set aside.

2 Heat the oil in a wok, add the red curry paste, and fry, stirring, for *30 seconds*. Add 3 tablespoons of the coconut milk, mix it with the paste, then add the remainder and stir over a gentle heat for *1 minute*.

3 Add the duck and stir for *2 minutes*. Add the sugar, lime leaves, peas, chili, chicken stock, tomatoes, and pineapple. Mix well together and then, when the curry is simmering, add the *nam pla*. Stir well and transfer to a bowl. Serve with the extra pineapple and noodles, if liked, garnished with red pepper and green onion strips.

Serves 3–4

Phuket Chicken and Lemon Grass Curry

Preparation time: 15 minutes
Cooking time: about 1 hour

- 3 tablespoons vegetable oil
- 4 garlic cloves, crushed
- 3 shallots, chopped
- 3 lemon grass stalks,
  very finely chopped, or ¾
  teaspoon grated lemon rind
- 6 kaffir lime leaves,
  shredded, or ¼ teaspoon
  grated lime rind
- 3 tablespoons Green Curry
  Paste (see page 8)

- 1 tablespoon *nam pla* (fish
  sauce)
- 2 teaspoons palm sugar
  (jaggery) or light brown sugar
- 1 cup Chicken Stock (see
  page 7)
- 8 large chicken drumsticks

TO GARNISH:
- 1 red chili, sliced
- kaffir lime leaves (optional)
- lemon grass stalks (optional)

1 Heat the oil in a large, flameproof casserole, add the garlic and shallots, and fry over a gentle heat, stirring, for *3 minutes,* or until softened.

2 Add the lemon grass, lime leaves, green curry paste, *nam pla,* and sugar to the pan. Fry for *1 minute,* then add the stock and chicken drumsticks and bring the curry to a boil. Reduce the heat, cover the pan, and simmer the curry gently, stirring occasionally, for *40–45 minutes,* until the chicken is tender and cooked through.

3 Taste and adjust the seasoning, if necessary. Serve the curry hot, garnished with chili slices, lime leaves, and knotted lemon grass stalks, if using. Noodles would be a good accompaniment to this curry.

Serves 4

Spicy Chicken Satay

Preparation time: 15 minutes, plus marinating
Cooking time: 30–35 minutes

- 8 chicken wing joints
- salt and pepper
- 1 teaspoon palm sugar
  (jaggery) or light brown sugar

SPICY MARINADE:

- 1 tablespoon ground almonds
- 1 tablespoon ground ginger
- 1 teaspoon ground cilantro
- pinch of chili powder
- 1 teaspoon turmeric
- 1¼ cups Coconut Milk (see
  page 8)
- 1 small red bell pepper,
  seeded and finely chopped

SATAY SAUCE:

- 2 onions, coarsely chopped
- 1¼ cups peanuts, roasted
  (see page 8)
- pinch of chili powder
- 2 tablespoons oil
- ½ cup water
- 1 teaspoon sugar
- 1 tablespoon soy sauce
- 2 tablespoons lemon juice

TO SERVE:

- lemon wedges
- 1 red and 1 yellow bell
  pepper, finely diced

TO GARNISH:

- chopped fresh cilantro
- bay leaves (optional)

1 Sprinkle the chicken with salt and pepper and place in a shallow dish. To make the marinade, mix together the ground almonds, ginger, cilantro, chili, and turmeric in a bowl, then gradually add the coconut milk. Stir in the red bell pepper, then pour the mixture over the chicken and leave to marinate for about *2 hours*.

2 Meanwhile, make the satay sauce. Place half of the chopped onions in a blender or food processor, add the peanuts and chili powder, and process until the mixture is reduced to a paste. Heat the oil in a saucepan, add the remaining onions, and sauté until soft. Add the peanut paste and cook, stirring, for *3 minutes*. Gradually add the water, stirring all the time. Stir in the sugar and cook for *5 minutes*. Add the soy sauce and lemon juice and stir. Keep hot.

3 Drain the chicken and reserve the marinade. Sprinkle with the brown sugar and cook under a preheated hot broiler for *15–20 minutes*, until the chicken is cooked and crisp. Turn the pieces frequently and baste with the marinade. Serve the pieces with the lemon wedges, diced bell peppers and, in a separate small bowl, the satay sauce. Garnish with chopped fresh cilantro and bay leaves, if using.

Serves 4

Pork Satay

Preparation time: 15–20 minutes, plus marinating
Cooking time: 45 minutes

- 1 lb pork loin
- 1 teaspoon salt
- 2 teaspoons palm sugar (jaggery) or light brown sugar
- 1 teaspoon ground turmeric
- 1 teaspoon ground cilantro
- 1 teaspoon ground cumin
- ¾ cup Coconut Milk (see page 8)
- chili powder, for sprinkling
- cilantro sprigs, to garnish
- lemon slices, to serve

PEANUT SAUCE:
- ⅓ cup peanuts, roasted (see page 8)
- 1 teaspoon salt
- 1¼ cups Coconut Milk (see page 8)
- 2 teaspoons Red Curry Paste (see page 7)
- 2 tablespoons sugar
- ½ teaspoon lemon juice

1 Cut the pork into 2-inch strips and place in a large bowl. Add the salt, sugar, turmeric, cilantro, cumin, and 4 tablespoons of the coconut milk. Mix thoroughly, using clean hands to knead the spices into the meat. Cover and leave to marinate for at least *2 hours*.

2 To make the sauce, grind the peanuts with the salt in a mortar until the mixture turns into a thick cream. Set aside. Put half the coconut milk in a saucepan with the curry paste. Heat gently for *3 minutes*, stirring constantly. Stir in the ground peanuts with the sugar, lemon juice, and remaining coconut milk. Simmer gently for *20–30 minutes*, stirring often to prevent the sauce from sticking. Transfer to a bowl.

3 Thread the marinated pork onto oiled skewers and cook on a barbecue or under a preheated hot broiler for *12–15 minutes*, turning them several times and brushing frequently with the reserved coconut milk. Sprinkle the kebabs with chili powder, garnish with sprigs of cilantro, and serve with the peanut sauce and some lemon slices.

Serves 4

Pork with Hot Sauces

Preparation time: 15 minutes
Cooking time: 8–10 minutes

- 12 oz pork loin
- ½ teaspoon salt
- ¼ teaspoon white pepper
- 1 tablespoon butter
- 1 tablespoon oil
- 3 garlic cloves, peeled
- ½-inch piece of fresh root ginger, peeled and chopped
- 2 red chilies, chopped
- 1½ teaspoons ground cumin
- ½ cucumber, finely diced, to serve

CHILI AND GINGER SAUCE:
- 2 red chilies
- 1-inch piece of fresh root ginger, peeled and chopped
- ¼ cup grated onions
- salt

TOMATO AND CHILI SAUCE:
- 2 tomatoes, skinned and chopped
- 2 garlic cloves, crushed
- pinch of sugar
- 1 teaspoon hot chili powder
- salt

1 Slice the pork thinly and rub with salt and pepper. Heat the butter and oil in a wok or small frying pan over a moderate heat. Add the pork and stir-fry until lightly browned. Remove from the wok and keep warm.

2 Chop the garlic finely and add to the wok with the ginger, chilies, and cumin. Stir-fry for *2 minutes*, and then return the pork to the wok. Stir-fry for *2 minutes* over low heat, or until the meat is tender. If necessary, add a sprinkling of water to keep the meat moist.

3 To make the chili and ginger sauce, put the chilies, ginger, onions, and salt in a mortar and pound to a smooth paste.

4 To make the tomato and chili sauce, put the chopped tomatoes and garlic in a small bowl, then mix in a good pinch of sugar, the hot chili powder, and salt to taste. Serve the stir-fried pork with the cucumber and two hot sauces.

Serves 4

variation _____

Beef with Hot Sauces

Preparation time: 15 minutes
Cooking time: about 10 minutes

1 Substitute 12 oz loin steak for the pork. Slice the steak thinly and rub with salt and pepper. Heat the butter and oil in a wok or small frying pan over a moderate heat. Add the steak and stir-fry very briefly, just until lightly browned. Remove from the wok and keep warm.

2 Chop the garlic finely and add to the wok with the ginger, chilies, and cumin. Stir-fry for *2 minutes*, and then return the steak to the wok. Stir-fry for *1 minute* over a low heat, or until the meat is tender. If necessary, add a sprinkling of water to keep the meat moist.

3 Follow steps 3 and 4 of the main recipe to make the two hot sauces and serve with the steak.

Thai Green Beef Curry

Preparation time: 10 minutes
Cooking time: 25 minutes

- 2 tablespoons peanut oil
- 1-inch piece of fresh root ginger, finely chopped
- 2 shallots, chopped
- 4 tablespoons Green Curry Paste (see page 8)
- 1 lb loin steak, cubed
- 1¼ cups Coconut Milk (see page 8)
- 4 tablespoons *nam pla* (fish sauce)
- 1 teaspoon palm sugar (jaggery) or light brown sugar

- 3 kaffir lime leaves, finely chopped, or ¼ teaspoon grated lime rind
- 2 teaspoons tamarind water (see page 68)
- 1 green chili, seeded and finely sliced
- salt and pepper
- boiled rice, to serve

TO GARNISH:

- yellow bell pepper strips
- fried chopped garlic
- red chili strip, curled (optional)

1 Heat the oil in a wok. Add the ginger and shallots and stir-fry over a low heat for about *3 minutes,* or until softened. Add the green curry paste and fry for *2 minutes*.

2 Add the steak to the wok, stir until evenly coated in the spice mixture, and fry for *3 minutes* to seal the meat. Stir in the coconut milk and bring to a boil. Reduce the heat and cook the curry over a low heat, stirring occasionally, for about *10 minutes,* or until the beef is cooked through and the sauce has thickened.

3 Stir in the *nam pla*, sugar, lime leaves, tamarind water, and chili. Cook the curry for a further *5 minutes*, then season to taste.

4 Serve the curry hot with rice, garnished with yellow bell pepper strips and fried garlic, and topped with a red chili curl, if liked.

Beef and Galangal Salad

Preparation time: 10 minutes
Cooking time: 20–25 minutes

- 2 tablespoons glutinous rice
- 10 oz ground beef
- 5 thin slices galangal or fresh root ginger
- 3 tablespoons finely chopped green onion (scallion)
- 1 teaspoon ground chili
- 3–4 tablespoons lemon juice
- 3 tablespoons *nam pla* (fish sauce)
- ½ teaspoon sugar
- 4–5 mint sprigs, leaves chopped
- 3 tablespoons chopped shallots
- 1 crisp lettuce, separated into leaves, to serve
- mint sprigs, to garnish

1 Place the glutinous rice in a saucepan over moderate heat and dry-fry, stirring constantly, for *10 minutes*, or until the grains turn light brown. Remove from the heat. Grind in a blender or food processor, or pound using a pestle and mortar until the rice is very fine.

2 Put the ground beef in a saucepan and cook over a gentle heat for *10–15 minutes*, stirring constantly, until the meat has been cooked and all the liquid has been absorbed. Transfer to a mixing bowl and stir in the ground rice. Add the galangal, green onion, ground chili, lemon juice, *nam pla*, sugar, mint, and shallots to the mixing bowl, and mix well.

3 Arrange a bed of lettuce on a shallow dish and top with the beef mixture. Garnish with mint sprigs and serve at once.

Serves 4

Chiang Mai Jungle Curry with Beef

The fiery flavors of this curry are typical of northern Thailand. Although this version uses beef, jungle dishes from northern Thailand often contain more exotic meats such as monkey or even snake!

Preparation time: 15 minutes
Cooking time: about 1 hour

- 2 tablespoons peanut oil
- 1 lb lean beef, thinly sliced
- 1⅔ cups Coconut Milk (see page 8)
- salt and pepper

SPICE PASTE:

- 2 tablespoons yellow bean sauce
- 3 tablespoons Red Curry Paste (see page 7)
- 2 tablespoons palm sugar (jaggery) or light brown sugar
- 4 shallots, chopped
- 2 garlic cloves, chopped

- 2 large red chilies, seeded and chopped
- 1 lemon grass stalk, chopped, or ¼ teaspoon grated lemon rind
- 1-inch piece of galangal or fresh root ginger, chopped
- ½ teaspoon Thai shrimp paste
- 4 tablespoons lime juice

TO GARNISH:

- ½ red bell pepper, cut into thin strips
- 2 green onions (scallions), shredded

1 Place the ingredients for the spice paste in a food processor or blender and work to a thick paste. Alternatively, pound using a pestle and mortar.

2 Heat the oil in a large, flameproof casserole, add the beef, and stir-fry over a moderate heat for *3 minutes* to seal the meat. Stir in the paste and stir-fry for a further *3 minutes*. Pour the coconut milk into the casserole, stir to mix, and bring to a boil. Reduce the heat, cover the casserole dish, and simmer the curry gently, stirring occasionally, for *50 minutes,* or until the beef is tender. Season to taste.

3 Serve the curry hot with rice, garnished with strips of red bell pepper and the green onions.

Serves 3

Beef and Bamboo Shoot Salad

Preparation time: 15 minutes
Cooking time: 10–15 minutes

- 7 oz sirloin steak, thinly sliced
- 1 cup Coconut Milk (see page 8)
- 2 cups canned bamboo shoots, sliced
- 1½ tablespoons Red Curry Paste (see page 7)
- 2 tablespoons chopped lemon grass stalk (optional)
- 1½ teaspoons finely grated lemon rind
- 2 tablespoons lemon juice

- 1½ teaspoons *nam pla* (fish sauce)
- 3 small Thai chilies, finely chopped, or ½ teaspoon ground chili
- 1 lettuce, separated into leaves, to serve

TO GARNISH:
- 1 red chili, finely sliced
- green onion (scallion) strips
- finely sliced kaffir lime leaves (optional)

1 Place the steak in a small saucepan with the coconut milk and cook over a low heat for *10–15 minutes*, or until the steak is tender and has absorbed most of the coconut milk. (Any liquid remaining in the pan should have an oily appearance.) Remove the pan from the heat and set aside until the meat is cool.

2 Transfer the meat to a bowl. Add the remaining ingredients, except the lettuce, and mix well.

3 Arrange a bed of lettuce on a shallow serving dish, top with the beef mixture, and garnish with the chili, green onion, and sliced lime leaves, if using. Serve immediately.

Serves 4

Fish and Seafood

This chapter offers a wide variety of ways to prepare fresh fish and seafood, using a wonderful array of herbs and spices. There are, of course, the usual spicy curries aplenty but also more subtle sauces which accentuate delicate flavors and textures, giving a distinctly Thai feel to everything from mussels to mackerel.

Thai Red Shrimp and Cucumber Curry

Preparation time: 10 minutes
Cooking time: 15 minutes

- 2 tablespoons peanut oil
- 1 shallot, chopped
- 2 garlic cloves, chopped
- 2 tablespoons Red Curry Paste (see page 7)
- 1 red chili, seeded and chopped
- 3 kaffir lime leaves, finely shredded, or ¼ teaspoon grated lime rind
- 1¼ cups Coconut Milk (see page 8)

- 20 raw large shrimp, peeled and deveined
- ¼ cucumber, halved lengthways, seeded, and thickly sliced
- 1 tablespoon *nam pla* (fish sauce)
- 1 teaspoon palm sugar (jaggery) or light brown sugar
- noodles, to serve

TO GARNISH:
- shredded kaffir lime leaves
- cucumber ribbons

1 Heat the oil in a wok, add the shallot and garlic, and fry over a gentle heat, stirring, for about *3 minutes* until softened. Add the red curry paste, chili, and lime leaves and fry for a further *1 minute*.

2 Add the coconut milk, increase the heat, and bring the sauce to a boil, then reduce the heat and simmer the sauce gently, stirring occasionally, for *5 minutes*.

3 Add the shrimp, cucumber, *nam pla*, and sugar to the wok. Stir to coat the ingredients evenly in the sauce, then simmer the curry gently for *5 minutes,* or until the shrimp have turned pink and are cooked through and the cucumber is tender. Taste and adjust the seasoning, if necessary. Serve the curry hot with noodles, garnished with shredded lime leaves and cucumber ribbons, if liked.

Serves 4

Spicy Shrimp Curry

Preparation time: 10 minutes, plus chilling
Cooking time: 30–35 minutes

- 3¼ cups Coconut Milk (see page 8)
- 2 tablespoons Green Curry Paste (see page 8)
- 2 teaspoons ground galangal or ginger
- 1¼ lb raw large shrimp
- 2 tablespoons *nam pla* (fish sauce)
- rice, to serve

TO GARNISH:
- 1 tablespoon green chili, cut into 1-inch strips
- 4 basil leaves, shredded

1 Put the coconut milk in a jug and chill in the refrigerator for at least 1 hour, or until the thick milk rises to the surface. Scoop about a third of the coconut milk off the top and put it into a wok or heavy saucepan. Reserve the remaining coconut milk for later.

2 Bring the thick coconut milk to a boil and then simmer, uncovered, stirring occasionally, until the coconut oil begins to bubble to the surface and the liquid reduces to a quarter of its original volume. Add the curry paste and galangal and bring to a boil. Cook over a medium to high heat until most of the liquid evaporates.

3 Shell and devein the shrimp and wash them under cold running water. Pat dry and add to the mixture in the wok. Stir-fry for 3–4 minutes until they are firm and pink.

4 Stir in the remaining coconut milk and the *nam pla* and simmer for 6–8 minutes, stirring occasionally. Serve garnished with strips of green chili and basil leaves, and accompanied by rice, if liked.

Serves 4–6

Thai Garnishes

Renowned for its appeal to the eye as well as to the palate, Thai cuisine places as much importance on food presentation as on the meal itself. The garnishes shown here are very simple but delightfully effective in adding to the overall look and flavor of your dish.

Cucumber and tomato in chili oil

Shredded kaffir lime leaves

Yellow bell pepper strips

Julienne of carrot

Green onion (scallion) strips

Red bell pepper strips

Red and yellow bell pepper strips and dice provide vibrant color and crisp freshness to many Thai meals, particularly creamy dishes. Finely sliced small shards may also be sprinkled over soups and curries.

Diced cucumber and tomato in chili oil works as both a refreshing side-dish or *sambal* for spicy curries, and as a colorful and tasty dipping sauce for finger snacks.
Julienne of carrot is finely cut carrot strips, used to add brightness and a delicate texture to vegetable dishes and salads.
Shredded kaffir lime leaves sprinkled over a variety of dishes give a sharp citrus edge, and are used frequently in Thai cuisine to complement a whole range of flavors.
Green onion (scallion) strips provide a crisp texture and strong taste to doughy snacks and salads. Thai cooks sprinkle finely chopped curls over fish and seafood dishes.

Fresh flowering chives

Red onion slivers

Red chili curls

Coconut shavings

Cucumber strips

Yellow bell pepper dice

Lime rind

Red bell pepper dice

Lime rind offers an alternative to kaffir lime leaves if these are unavailable.
Cucumber strips are strips of cucumber that have been sliced down the cucumber's entire length, and can then be skewered and bunched to form a ribbon. Cucumber offsets the spiciness of Thai dishes, and may also be finely diced and sprinkled.
Fresh flowering chives are similar in taste to ordinary chives but with an edible bud, which adds a fresh, natural look to the presented dish.
Red onion slivers are used to add a vivid pinkish color and crisp texture to soups, salads, and creamy curries.
Coconut shavings provide the perfect finish to most Thai meals, adding a cool sweetness to hot dishes and desserts alike.
Red chili curls are striking in color and shape, and when sprinkled over soups, curries, and salads give them a vivid appearance, as well as adding a final touch of spice.

Mussels with Thai Herbs

Preparation time: 20 minutes
Cooking time: 20 minutes

- 4 lb fresh mussels
- 5 cups water
- 6 kaffir lime leaves or
  ½ teaspoon grated lime rind
- rind of 1 lemon
- 2 lemon grass stalks

- 1 tablespoon salt
- 3 red chilies, sliced
- 3 green onions (scallions),
  chopped
- cilantro leaves, to garnish

1 Clean the mussels thoroughly and remove the beards.
Tap any open shells to ensure that they close. If not, throw
those mussels away.

2 Pour the water into a large saucepan and bring to a boil.
Add the lime leaves, lemon rind, lemon grass, and salt. Then
add the mussels, cover the pan, and bring back to a boil.

3 Cook the mussels, shaking the pan occasionally, until they
open. Drain them, reserving half of the cooking liquid. Transfer
the mussels to a deep serving dish, throwing away any that
have not opened.

4 Strain the reserved liquid, discarding the lime leaves,
lemon rind, and lemon grass. Bring to a boil, add the sliced
red chilies and green onions, and then boil vigorously for
2 minutes. Pour over the mussels and serve immediately,
garnished with cilantro leaves.

Serves 4

Fresh Crab Curry with Chilies

To prepare the crabmeat, remove the legs and claws from the crab and set aside. Remove the undershell and discard the gills. Clean the body of the crab and cut the meat into small chunks. Crack the legs and claws, extract the meat, and set aside with the rest of the meat.

Preparation time: 15 minutes
Cooking time: 15–20 minutes

- 1 teaspoon curry powder
- 1 cup water
- 1 lb dressed crabmeat (see above)
- 4 green onions (scallions), chopped
- 2 red chilies, seeded and finely sliced
- 1½ teaspoons sugar

- 1 tablespoon white wine
- ½ teaspoon salt
- ¼ teaspoon pepper
- 1 egg
- 1 tablespoon light cream

TO SERVE:
- dried mango slices
- shrimp crackers
- sliced red chilies

1 Mix the curry powder with the water in a saucepan and bring to a boil.

2 Stir in the crabmeat. Allow the liquid to return to a boil and add the green onions, chilies, sugar, wine, salt, and pepper. Lower the heat and simmer for *10 minutes*.

3 Meanwhile, combine the egg and cream in a small bowl. Mix well, beat in 2 tablespoons of the curry sauce, and return the mixture to the saucepan. Stir over a gentle heat for *1 minute*, transfer to a serving bowl or even a clean crab shell, if you like, and garnish with dried mango slices, shrimp crackers, and extra chili slices.

Serves 4

Shrimp in Coconut Sauce

Preparation time: 20 minutes
Cooking time: 20 minutes

- 16 raw large shrimp
- 2 tablespoons oil
- 1 large onion, finely chopped
- 2 lemon grass stalks, chopped, or ¼ teaspoon grated lemon rind
- 2 red chilies, sliced
- 1-inch piece of fresh root ginger, shredded
- 1 tablespoon ground cumin
- 1 tablespoon ground cilantro
- 2 tablespoons *nam pla* (fish sauce)

- 1 cup thick Coconut Milk (see page 8)
- 3 tablespoons Crushed Roasted Nuts (see page 8)
- 2 tomatoes, skinned and chopped
- 1 teaspoon sugar
- lemon grass stalks, to garnish (optional)

TO SERVE:
- 1 tablespoon lime juice
- cilantro leaves, chopped

1 Remove the shrimp from their shells, leaving the tails intact. Remove the dark veins running along the back of the shrimp.

2 Heat the oil in a wok or heavy frying pan. Add the onion and fry until soft and golden. Add the chopped lemon grass, sliced red chilies, ginger, cumin, and cilantro and sauté for *2 minutes*.

3 Add the *nam pla* and coconut milk to the wok. Stir well, and then add the nuts and chopped tomatoes. Cook gently over a low heat until the tomatoes are soft and the flavors of the sauce are well developed.

4 Stir in the shrimp and simmer gently for *5 minutes,* or until they are pink and tender. Add the sugar, and then transfer the shrimp to a warm serving dish. Serve hot, sprinkled with lime juice and chopped cilantro leaves, garnished with lemon grass stalks, if liked.

Serves 4

variation _____

Chicken in Coconut Sauce

Preparation time: 20 minutes
Cooking time: 20–25 minutes

1 Substitute 12 oz of boneless, skinless chicken breast for the shrimp. Slice the chicken across the grain into thin, bite-sized pieces. Heat the oil in a wok or heavy frying pan and stir-fry the chicken for *2–3 minutes*, until lightly browned. Remove the chicken from the wok and keep warm.

2 Add the onion to the wok and fry until soft and golden. Add the chopped lemon grass, sliced red chilies, ginger, cumin, and cilantro and sauté for *2 minutes*.

3 Add the *nam pla* and coconut milk to the wok. Stir well, and then add the nuts and chopped tomatoes. Cook gently over a low heat until the tomatoes are soft and the flavors of the sauce are well developed.

4 Stir in the chicken and simmer gently for *5–8 minutes*, or until tender and cooked completely through. Add the sugar, and then transfer the chicken to a warm serving dish. Serve hot, sprinkled with lime juice and chopped cilantro leaves.

Broiled Fish in Ginger and Oyster Sauce

Preparation time: 20 minutes
Cooking time: 20 minutes

- 1 gray mullet, cleaned
- ½ tablespoon Garlic Mixture
  (see page 8)
- ½ cup chopped onions
- 5 mushrooms, sliced
- 2 tablespoons finely sliced
  fresh root ginger
- 1 celery stalk, sliced

- 1 teaspoon pepper
- 1 tablespoon soy sauce
- 1 tablespoon oyster sauce
- 1 cup Fish Stock (see page 7)
- lemon slices, to garnish

1 Score the skin of the mullet with a sharp knife to allow the sauce to be absorbed during cooking. Rub the fish with the garlic mixture, pressing it well into the cuts. Transfer the fish to a shallow, heatproof dish.

2 In a bowl, mix together the remaining ingredients and pour over the fish. Cook under a preheated broiler for *20 minutes*, turning the fish over halfway through the cooking time.

3 Carefully transfer the fish onto a warm serving dish, pour over the sauce, garnish with lemon slices, and serve.

Serves 2

Spicy Fishcakes

Preparation time: 20 minutes
Cooking time: 16–20 minutes

- 1 lb cod fillet, skinned and cut into chunks
- 3 tablespoons Red Curry Paste (see page 7)
- 1 egg
- 3 tablespoons *nam pla* (fish sauce)
- 1–2 tablespoons rice flour
- ⅔ cup thin green beans, finely chopped
- 1 tablespoon finely shredded kaffir lime leaves, or ¼ teaspoon grated lime rind
- oil, for deep-frying

TO SERVE:
- Chili Sauce (see page 22)
- lime slices

1 Put the cod and red curry paste in a food processor or blender. Process until the fish is pounded to a paste. Alternatively, pound in a mortar with a pestle.

2 Transfer the fish to a bowl. Add the egg, *nam pla*, and sufficient flour to knead with your hands into a stiff mixture. Work in the beans and lime leaves.

3 Form the fish mixture into 16–20 balls, and, using your hands, flatten each ball into a round, about ½-inch thick.

4 Heat the oil in a wok or large, deep frying pan and fry the fishcakes, a few at a time, for *4–5 minutes* on each side, until they are cooked and golden. Take care not to overcook them. Drain on paper towels and serve hot with chili sauce, slices of lime, and a cucumber salad, if wished.

Serves 4–5

variation
Spicy Shrimp Cakes

Preparation time: 20 minutes
Cooking time: 16–20 minutes

Replace half of the cod fillet with 8 oz raw large shrimp, shelled and deveined. Continue as for the main recipe.

Fish with Tamarind Water and Ginger

Tamarind paste is made from the dried, bitter pod of the tamarind tree, shaped into blocks, and is used as a souring agent in many South-east Asian dishes. To make tamarind water, place a 2 oz piece of paste in 1¼ cups of boiling water, leave to soften, then strain through a sieve until you have the required amount. Use distilled white vinegar or lemon juice as an alternative.

Preparation time: 20 minutes
Cooking time: 25 minutes

- 2 gray mullet or mackerel, cleaned
- 4 shallots, chopped
- 1 tablespoon Thai shrimp paste
- 1 teaspoon pepper
- 3¼ cups water
- 2 tablespoons finely chopped fresh root ginger, washed
- 2 tablespoons tamarind water
- 4 tablespoons *nam pla* (fish sauce)
- 3 tablespoons brown sugar
- 4 green onions (scallions), chopped, plus extra to garnish

TO SERVE:
- boiled rice
- cucumber slices
- pickled chilies (optional)

1 Remove the head and tail from each mullet or mackerel and cut the fish lengthways in half. Score the skin with a sharp knife to allow the sauce to be absorbed during cooking.

2 Grind the shallots with the Thai shrimp paste and pepper in a food processor or blender until the ingredients are thoroughly blended and the mixture forms a paste. Alternatively, pound to a paste using a pestle and mortar. Stir the paste into the water in a saucepan large enough to take the pieces of fish and bring to a boil.

3 Add the fish, ginger, tamarind water, *nam pla*, sugar and green onions. Lower the heat and simmer for about *20 minutes*. Serve hot with rice, cucumber slices, and pickled chilies, if liked, and garnished with chopped green onions.

Serves 4

Fish in Garlic Sauce

Preparation time: 15 minutes
Cooking time: 20 minutes

- 1 mullet, lemon sole, or porgy,
  cleaned
- oil, for deep-frying
- 3 tablespoons vegetable oil
- 2 tablespoons Garlic Mixture
  (see page 8)

- 2 tablespoons *nam pla* (fish
  sauce)
- 1 teaspoon sugar
- 2 celery stalks, thinly sliced

TO GARNISH:
- cilantro sprigs
- 1 red chili, thinly sliced

1 Neatly score the skin of the fish diagonally in both directions to allow the sauce to be absorbed during cooking. Pat dry with paper towels. Heat the oil in a wok or deep saucepan and deep-fry the fish for *10–15 minutes* until golden brown. Using a slotted spoon, carefully remove the fish from the wok or saucepan and drain on paper towels.

2 Meanwhile, heat the vegetable oil in a saucepan large enough to hold the fish in a single layer. Stir in the garlic mixture and cook until it changes color. Add the *nam pla* and stir in the sugar. Add the fish to the pan, turning it until well coated.

3 Transfer the fish to a serving dish and keep warm. Add the celery to the sauce remaining in the pan and stir-fry for *2 minutes*, then pour the mixture over the fish. Garnish with cilantro sprigs and strips of red chili. Serve warm.

Serves 4

Rice and Noodles

Rice and noodles are not only the perfect accompaniment to main dishes, but also the basis for several healthy and delicious meals themselves. Equally mouthwatering combined with meat, fish, or vegetables these versatile and nourishing foods are a vital part of any Thai meal.

Noodles with Fish Curry Topping

Preparation time: 20 minutes
Cooking time: 25 minutes
Oven temperature: 325°F

- 8 oz cod fillets
- 1 cup water
- 4 cups Coconut Milk (see page 8)
- 3 tablespoons Red Curry Paste (see page 7)
- 3 tablespoons *nam pla* (fish sauce)
- 7 oz noodles

- 1 cup green beans
- 2 cups bean sprouts
- ½ cup Coconut Cream (see page 8)

TO GARNISH:
- 1 red chili, seeded and finely sliced
- 2 tablespoons basil leaves

1 Place the fish in a saucepan with the measured water. Bring to a boil, lower the heat, and simmer for *8–10 minutes,* or until the fish flakes easily when tested with a fork. Remove the fish from the saucepan with a slotted spoon and reserve the stock. Discard the skin and flake the flesh.

2 Place the flaked fish in a clean saucepan with the coconut milk. Bring to just below the boiling point and stir in the reserved fish stock.

3 Add the red curry paste to the fish mixture, together with the *nam pla*. Simmer for *15 minutes*, stirring occasionally.

4 Meanwhile, bring 2 large saucepans of water to a boil. Add the noodles to the first and cook for *10 minutes*. For the last 3 minutes of cooking, add the green beans and bean sprouts to the second pan and boil for *2–3 minutes* and *1 minute* respectively. Drain all 3 ingredients thoroughly, rinse under cold running water and drain again. Scoop the noodles gently into loose nest shapes, transfer to a large serving plate with the green beans and bean sprouts, and keep warm in a preheated 325°F oven.

5 When the fish curry has thickened and a thin film of oil appears on the surface, stir in the coconut cream. Bring to a boil, remove from the heat, and spoon the curry over the noodles. Serve immediately, with the green beans and bean sprouts, and garnished with chili and basil leaves.

Serves 4

Rice Vermicelli in Coconut Milk

Preparation time: 15 minutes, plus soaking
Cooking time: 45 minutes

- 8 oz rice vermicelli
- 2 teaspoons oil
- 2 eggs, beaten
- 2 cups Coconut Milk (see page 8)
- ½ cup roughly chopped onions
- 8 oz raw large shrimp, shelled
- 4 tablespoons soy sauce
- 2 tablespoons sugar
- 1 tablespoon lemon juice
- 4–5 cups bean sprouts
- ¾ cup chopped green onions (scallions)

TO GARNISH:

- 3 tablespoons chopped cilantro leaves
- 2 red chilies, seeded and sliced

1 Soak the vermicelli in a bowl of warm water for *15–20 minutes*. Bring a large saucepan of water to the boil, add the soaked vermicelli, and cook, stirring occasionally, for *15 minutes*. Drain the vermicelli well and set aside.

2 Heat the oil in an omelet pan or small frying pan and add the eggs. Tilt the pan to form an omelet, lifting the sides of the omelet to allow any uncooked egg mixture to flow underneath. Remove the cooked, set omelet from the pan and slice into thin shreds. Keep warm.

3 In a large wok or saucepan, bring the coconut milk to a boil. Cook over a high heat for *10 minutes*, until a film of oil forms on top. Stir in the onions, shrimp, soy sauce, sugar, and lemon juice. Cook for *5 minutes*, and then transfer half of the mixture to a bowl and keep warm.

4 Add the reserved vermicelli to the mixture in the wok. Mix well, and then cook for *5 minutes*. Stir in half of the bean sprouts and green onions. Pile the vermicelli mixture onto a serving dish and top with the reserved shrimp mixture and shredded omelet. Garnish with cilantro and chilies, and serve with the remaining bean sprouts and green onions.

Serves 4

Shrimp Vermicelli

Preparation time: 10 minutes
Cooking time: 20 minutes

- ½ cup milk
- 1 teaspoon dark soy sauce
- 3 tablespoons oyster sauce
- 2 tablespoons vegetable oil
- 1 teaspoon chopped garlic
- 5 black peppercorns, crushed
- 1 tablespoon cilantro leaf, stem, and root
- ¾-inch piece of fresh root ginger, peeled and shredded

- 4 oz bean thread vermicelli or cellophane noodles, soaked
- 12 raw large shrimp, shelled, but tails left intact
- 2 tablespoons Fish Stock (see page 7) or water, if needed
- cilantro leaves, to garnish

1 Combine the milk, soy sauce, and oyster sauce in a bowl.

2 Heat the oil in a wok, add the garlic, peppercorns, cilantro, and ginger and stir-fry for *30 seconds*. Add the vermicelli or noodles and the milk mixture, stir together thoroughly over a high heat, then reduce the heat to low, cover the wok, and cook for *12 minutes*.

3 Finally, turn the heat up, add the shrimp, and the fish stock, if the sauce looks too thick, and cook, stirring for about *2–3 minutes*, until all the shrimp have turned pink.

4 Turn into a serving bowl and garnish with cilantro leaves.

Serves 3–4

Egg-fried Noodles

Preparation time: 10 minutes
Cooking time: 20 minutes

- 4 tablespoons peanut oil
- 1 garlic clove, crushed
- 1 shallot or small onion, thinly sliced
- 4 oz fresh egg noodles
- grated rind of 1 lime
- 2 teaspoons soy sauce
- 2 tablespoons lime juice
- 4 oz chicken breast or pork loin, sliced
- 4 oz crabmeat or prepared squid
- 4 oz shelled raw shrimp

- 1 tablespoon yellow soybean paste
- 1 tablespoon *nam pla* (fish sauce)
- 2 tablespoons palm sugar (jaggery) or light brown sugar
- 2 eggs
- 2 red chilies, seeded and chopped
- pepper

TO GARNISH:
- cilantro leaves
- lime rind, finely sliced

1 Heat half of the oil in a wok or heavy frying pan. Add the garlic and the shallot and stir-fry quickly until golden and tender.

2 Plunge the egg noodles into boiling water for a few seconds. Drain well, and then add to the wok. Stir-fry with the grated lime rind, soy sauce, and lime juice for *3–4 minutes*. Remove, drain, and keep warm.

3 Add the remaining oil to the wok together with the chicken or pork, crabmeat or squid, and the shrimp. Stir-fry over a high heat until cooked. Season with pepper, and then stir in the soybean paste, *nam pla*, and sugar.

4 Break the eggs into the wok and stir gently until the mixture sets. Add the chilies and check the seasoning. Mix in the noodles and heat through over a low heat. Serve garnished with cilantro leaves and lime rind.

Serves 4

Spicy Fried Rice

Preparation time: 10 minutes, plus marinating
Cooking time: 10 minutes

- 4 oz ground beef
- 1 cup canned red kidney beans, drained
- 1½ tablespoons *nam pla* (fish sauce)
- 1 tablespoon dark soy sauce
- 4 red chilies, seeded and finely chopped
- 3 garlic cloves, crushed
- ½ teaspoon salt
- 2 tablespoons vegetable oil
- 10 green beans, trimmed and cut in ½-inch lengths
- 1½ lb boiled rice (about 6 oz raw weight)
- 1 tablespoon sugar
- salt and pepper
- *nam pla* (fish sauce) (optional)
- 4 tablespoons basil leaves
- finely chopped red bell pepper, to garnish

1 Put the ground beef and drained kidney beans in a bowl. Mix well, and then stir in the *nam pla* and soy sauce. Cover the bowl and set aside for *30 minutes* to allow the different flavors to blend.

2 Mix together the chilies, garlic, and salt in another bowl. Heat the oil in a wok or large frying pan, and then add the chili mixture. Stir-fry briskly for *1 minute*.

3 Add the beef and kidney bean mixture to the wok and cook, stirring constantly, for *3 minutes*, or until the beef is lightly browned. Add the green beans and stir-fry for *3 minutes* more over a moderate heat.

4 Stir in the cooked rice and sugar and cook, stirring, until the rice is hot and all the ingredients are thoroughly mixed. Add salt and pepper or *nam pla* to taste, if necessary. Mix in the basil leaves and transfer to a serving dish. Garnish with chopped red bell pepper.

Serves 4

Noodles with Chicken and Shrimp

Preparation time: 10 minutes
Cooking time: 20 minutes

- **4 tablespoons vegetable oil**
- **2 garlic cloves, crushed**
- **4 oz fresh thread egg noodles**
- **2 tablespoons dark soy sauce**
- **4 oz mixed raw sliced chicken breast, prepared squid, and shelled shrimp**
- **½ teaspoon pepper**

- **2 tablespoons *nam pla* (fish sauce)**
- **2 cups mixed shredded cabbage and broccoli florets**
- **1¼ cups Chicken Stock (see page 7)**
- **1 tablespoon cornstarch**
- **2 tablespoons sugar**

1 Heat half of the oil in a wok or large, deep frying pan. Add half the garlic and stir-fry for *1 minute* until golden brown. Add the noodles and 1 tablespoon of soy sauce and cook, stirring constantly, for *3–5 minutes*. Transfer to a serving dish and keep warm.

2 Heat the remaining oil in the wok and add the rest of the garlic. Stir-fry for *1 minute* until golden brown. Add the chicken breast, squid, shrimp, pepper, and *nam pla*. Stir-fry for *5 minutes*.

3 Add the shredded cabbage and broccoli florets to the meat and seafood mixture in the wok and stir-fry for *3 minutes*.

4 Stir in the stock. Mix the cornstarch with 2 tablespoons of water and stir into the wok. Add the remaining soy sauce and the sugar and bring to a boil. Lower the heat and cook for *3 minutes*, stirring constantly. Pour the thickened sauce over the noodles and serve immediately.

Serves 4

Crispy Noodles

Preparation time: 6 minutes
Cooking time: 35 minutes

- 1½ oz tamarind pod, soaked and squeezed into 1¼ cups hot water (see page 68)
- 1⅓ cups palm sugar (jaggery) or light brown sugar
- 6 tablespoons tomato ketchup
- 3 tablespoons *nam pla* (fish sauce)
- oil, for deep-frying
- 4 oz rice vermicelli
- 1½ oz fried tofu cut into 1-inch x ¼-inch pieces
- green onion (scallion) tops, sliced, to garnish

1 Heat the tamarind water in a wok and melt the sugar in it— it will foam up. Add the ketchup and stir for *1 minute*, then add the *nam pla*. Cook, stirring, for *20–25 minutes*—the sauce will gradually thicken until it is almost the consistency of jam. Remove it from the heat and allow it to cool down a little.

2 In another wok, heat the oil until it is hot enough to deep-fry the noodles, and then drop them in, a handful at a time. They will puff up and expand immediately; remove them with a slotted spoon onto paper towels to drain.

3 When all the noodles are fried, put them into a large bowl and drizzle the sweet red sauce over them, working it in carefully with your hands until the crispy white noodles turn a pinky-brown. Pour off all but 1 tablespoon of the oil from the wok and reserve it for another time. Arrange the noodles on a serving dish.

4 Quickly fry the tofu pieces in the wok, then arrange them on top of the noodles. Sprinkle with the sliced green onion tops to garnish.

Serves 3–4

variation _____

Crispy Noodles with Duck

Preparation time: 10 minutes
Cooking time: 35 minutes

1 Follow steps 1–3 of the main recipe to make the sauce, deep-fry the noodles, and arrange them on a serving dish.

2 Substitute ¼ roast duck for the tofu. Remove the skin and meat from the bones and cut into bite-sized pieces. Quickly fry the duck in the wok to heat through, then arrange on top of the noodles. Sprinkle with sliced green onion tops.

Fried Noodles with Chicken and Broccoli

Preparation time: 10 minutes
Cooking time: 6–7 minutes

- 1½ tablespoons oil
- 1 large garlic clove, chopped
- 3 tablespoons chopped onions
- 4 oz boneless, skinless chicken breast, chopped
- 1 egg
- 5 oz rice noodles, soaked
- 1½ tablespoons palm sugar (jaggery) or light brown sugar
- 1 tablespoon tamarind water or distilled white vinegar

- 5 tablespoons light soy sauce
- 1⅓ cups broccoli florets and stalks
- 1 tablespoon chopped red bell pepper
- ½ cup chopped green onions (scallions)
- 1 cup bean sprouts
- 2 tablespoons Crushed Roasted Nuts (see page 8)
- ½ teaspoon pepper
- cilantro leaves, to garnish

1 Heat the oil in a wok, add the garlic, onions, and chopped chicken, and stir-fry over a high heat for *1 minute*.

2 Lower the heat, then break the egg into the mixture, stirring constantly. Add the noodles, sugar, tamarind water, soy sauce, and broccoli and cook, stirring, for *2 minutes*.

3 Add the remaining ingredients, turn the heat up, and stir-fry vigorously for about *1 minute*. Turn into a serving dish and garnish with cilantro leaves.

Serves 4

Noodle Salad

Preparation time: 10 minutes
Cooking time: 20 minutes
Oven temperature: 325°F

- **7 oz noodles**

FISH BALLS:

- **10 oz cod fillets, cooked and flaked**
- **1 tablespoon Red Curry Paste (see page 7)**
- **1 tablespoon chopped cilantro**
- **1 teaspoon salt**
- **1 tablespoon water**
- **1 cup Coconut Milk (see page 8)**
- **4 tablespoons *nam pla* (fish sauce)**
- **4 teaspoons sugar**

TO SERVE:

- **2-inch piece of fresh root ginger, peeled and thinly sliced**
- **3 garlic cloves, thinly sliced**
- **2 tablespoons minced shrimp**

TO GARNISH:

- **⅓ red, ⅓ yellow, and ⅓ green bell pepper, sliced into strips**
- **1 tablespoon finely sliced fresh root ginger**
- **sprig of cilantro**

1 Bring a large saucepan of water to the boil, add the noodles, and cook for *10 minutes*. Drain thoroughly, rinse under cold water, and drain again. With clean hands, scoop the noodles gently into loose nest shapes, transfer to a large serving plate, and warm through in a preheated 325°F oven.

2 Make the fish balls by combining the cod, red curry paste, chopped cilantro, salt, and water in a mixing bowl. Form the mixture into 40 balls and set aside.

3 Bring the coconut milk to a boil in a medium saucepan and add the fish balls, a few at a time, so that the milk continues to boil. Cook for about *4–5 minutes*, turning over halfway through cooking. As each ball cooks, remove it with a slotted spoon and drain on a wire rack set over a tray. Allow to cool. Reserve the coconut milk.

4 Arrange the cooked fish balls on top of the noodles and sprinkle with the ginger, garlic, and minced shrimp. Combine the reserved coconut milk with the *nam pla* and sugar. Pour the spiced milk over the top of the fish balls and garnish with strips of red, yellow, and green bell pepper, sliced fresh root ginger, and a sprig of cilantro. Serve immediately.

Serves 4

variation

For a hotter version of this popular dish, add five small Thai chilies to the sauce.

Vermicelli Noodles with Sauce

Preparation time: 10 minutes, plus soaking
Cooking time: 10 minutes

- 1 lb dried rice vermicelli
- 4 oz fried tofu, sliced
- 1 tablespoon Red Curry
  Paste (see page 7)
- 2 oz galangal or fresh root
  ginger, peeled and chopped
- 1 cup Coconut Milk (see
  page 8)

- 1½ teaspoons salt
- 1¼ cups hot water
- 2 teaspoons sugar

TO GARNISH:
- chopped cilantro leaves
- sliced fried tofu
- 1 red chili, finely sliced

1 Soak the rice vermicelli in a bowl of warm water for
15–20 minutes.

2 Meanwhile, put the tofu, red curry paste, galangal, coconut
milk, and salt in a blender or food processor and blend until
smooth. Add the hot water, and then blend again for
5 seconds. Pour the blended mixture into a saucepan and
bring to a boil, stirring continuously. Lower the heat to a
simmer, then add the sugar. Continue cooking gently for
3–4 minutes.

3 Drain the vermicelli and place in a serving bowl. Pour the
sauce over it and sprinkle with cilantro leaves, tofu slices, and
chili slices.

Serves 4–6

Coconut Rice

Preparation time: 10 minutes
Cooking time: 25 minutes

- 2 cups Coconut Milk (see
  page 8)
- ½ teaspoon turmeric
- 12 oz basmati rice, washed
  and drained
- 8 small onions, roughly
  chopped

- 20 peppercorns
- 1 teaspoon salt

TO GARNISH:
- green onions (scallions),
  finely chopped
- toasted coconut slivers
  (optional)

1 Put the coconut milk in a saucepan, stir in the turmeric,
then add the rice. Bring to a boil, then cover and simmer
gently for about *10 minutes*. Add the onions, peppercorns,
and salt and continue cooking gently for another *10 minutes*,
or until the rice is tender. Be careful not to let the rice burn.

2 Transfer to a warmed serving dish and garnish with
chopped green onions and coconut slivers, if liked.

Serves 4

Desserts

Though not the most obvious feature of the cuisine, Thai desserts are beautifully crafted and, like all Thai food, extremely appealing to both the eye and the palate. Exotic fruits such as papaya and mangoes are combined with staples such as rice and coconut to give a delightfully fresh yet decadent end to your Thai meal.

Coconut Cream Custard

Preparation time: 5 minutes
Cooking time: 15–20 minutes

- 2 large eggs
- 1 cup Coconut Milk (see page 8)
- 1 cup palm sugar (jaggery) or light brown sugar
- ¼ teaspoon salt
- 2 banana leaves (optional)
- shredded or freshly grated coconut, to decorate

1 Beat the eggs in a bowl, then add the coconut milk and sugar. Mix well, add the salt, and mix again.

2 Pour this mixture into 4 ramekins or, if you prefer, into banana leaf bowls (see variation).

3 Put the filled ramekins or banana leaf bowls into a steamer and steam for *15–20 minutes*. Serve warm, decorated with the coconut. If liked, wrap the ramekins in the banana leaves and tie with string.

Serves 4

variation _____

Coconut Cream Custard in Banana Leaf Bowls

Preparation time: 10 minutes

1 To give this dish a truly Thai feel, serve the custards in banana leaf bowls. To make the bowls, cut 8 equal-sized circles from the banana leaves and place 2 pieces together, shiny side out. Make 4 pleats opposite each other and secure with toothpicks to form a bowl. Make the remaining 3 bowls in the same way.

Sticky Rice with Mangoes

Preparation time: 20 minutes, plus soaking and cooling
Cooking time: 35–40 minutes

- **12 oz glutinous rice**
- **2½ cups Coconut Milk (see page 8)**
- **3 tablespoons sugar**
- **pinch of salt**
- **3 large ripe mangoes**
- **confectioners' sugar, for dusting**

SYRUP:
- **3 tablespoons palm sugar (jaggery) or light brown sugar**
- **3 tablespoons water**

1 Soak the glutinous rice in cold water overnight. The following day, drain the rice and put it in a large saucepan with the coconut milk, sugar, and salt. Bring slowly to a boil, then reduce the heat and simmer gently until all the coconut milk has been absorbed. Stir the mixture occasionally.

2 Put the cooked rice in the top of a foil-lined steamer and steam gently for *15–20 minutes* over simmering water. Press the rice into an oiled baking pan, spreading it out flat and pressing down hard. Set aside until it is firm and cooled. Using a pastry wheel, cut the rice into circles or slices.

3 Peel the mangoes and slice off the yellow flesh by standing the mangoes upright and cutting down on either side of the stone. Cut the flesh into thin slices or fans with a sharp knife.

4 To make the syrup, put the sugar in a small saucepan with the water. Heat gently over a low heat, stirring all the time until the sugar has completely dissolved. Arrange the rice circles or slices with the mango slices on a plate. Pour over a little of the sugar syrup and dust with confectioners' sugar.

Serves 6

Fresh Fruit Platter

In Thailand a selection of fresh fruit is the favorite end to a meal—the perfect way to cool and cleanse the palate after all those chilies!

Preparation time: 15–20 minutes

- **2 ripe mangoes**
- **1 small ripe papaya**
- **1 watermelon slice**

- **2 cups lychees, peeled**
- **1 lime, cut into quarters**

1 Peel and thickly slice the mangoes and papaya into 4 or 8 pieces. Cut the watermelon into chunks, removing as many of the seeds as you can.

2 Arrange all of the fruit on a serving plate and squeeze some lime juice over the papaya.

Serves 4

Bananas in Coconut Milk

Preparation time: 2 minutes
Cooking time: 10 minutes

- 1 cup Coconut Milk (see
  page 8)
- ¼ cup water
- 3 tablespoons palm sugar
  (jaggery) or light brown sugar

- 1 large or 2 small bananas,
  sliced diagonally
- rose petals, to decorate
  (optional)

1 Put the coconut milk, water, and sugar into a saucepan and simmer, stirring occasionally, for about *6 minutes*. Add the bananas and cook for *4 minutes* until heated through. Decorate with rose petals, if liked, but do not eat them.

Serves 2

Fried Apple and Coconut Cakes

Preparation time: 20 minutes, plus standing
Cooking time: 5–10 minutes

- ⅔ cup palm sugar (jaggery)
  or light brown sugar
- 1¾ cups water
- 2¼ cups rice flour
- 1 egg
- 2 teaspoons baking powder
- pinch of salt
- 1⅛ cups freshly grated
  coconut, or 2½ cups
  shredded coconut

- 4 apples
- oil, for deep-frying
- confectioners' sugar, for
  dusting

TO SERVE:

- crème fraîche or whipped
  heavy cream

1 Put the sugar and water in a saucepan and heat gently, stirring all the time until the sugar has dissolved. Bring to a boil, then stir gently for *2–3 minutes* until syrupy. Remove from the heat and set aside to cool.

2 Put the rice flour, egg, baking powder, salt, and coconut in a large mixing bowl. Mix all the ingredients together to form a smooth paste.

3 Pour in the cooled syrup and beat to make a smooth batter. Set aside for *20 minutes*. Core the apples and cut into rings, then add the rings to the batter.

4 Heat the oil in a heavy saucepan or wok and drop in some large spoonfuls of the fruit batter. Fry in batches until golden brown on both sides, turning once. Remove and drain on paper towels. Dust with confectioners' sugar and serve hot with crème fraîche or whipped heavy cream.

Serves 4

Special Photography:
Neil Mersh
Front Jacket Photography:
Philip Webb
Back Jacket Photography:
Neil Mersh
Other Photography:
Octopus Publishing Group Ltd.
/Jean Cazals /Sandra Lane
/James Merrell /Peter Myers
Special Photography Home
Economist: Sunil Vijayakar
Jacket Photography Home
Economist: Sunil Vijayakar

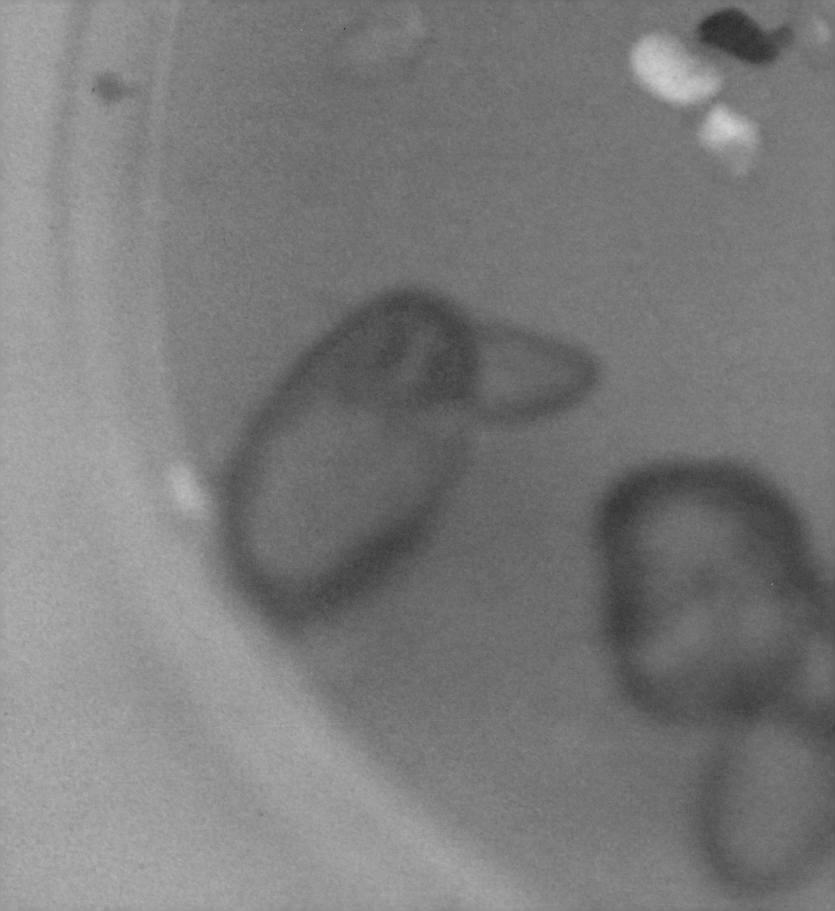